# VOODOO
## AN OUTSIDER'S GUIDE:
### Stories, Spells & Rituals

# Some Other Titles From New Falcon Publications

*Aha! The Sevenfold Mystery of the Ineffable Love*     **Aleister Crowley**
*An Insider's Guide to Robert Anton Wilson*     **Eric Wagner**
*Bio-Etheric Healing*     **Trudy Lanitis**
*Undoing Yourself With Energized Meditation and Other Devices, Secrets of Western Tantra: The Sexuality of the Middle Path, Dogma Daze*     **Christopher S. Hyatt, Ph.D.**
*Rebels & Devils; The Psychology of Liberation*     **Edited by Christopher S. Hyatt, Ph.D.**
*Aleister Crowley's Illustrated Goetia, Sex Magic, Tantra & Tarot: The Way of the Secret Lover, Taboo: Sex, Religion & Magick*     **C. S. Hyatt, Ph.D., and DuQuette**
*Pacts With The Devil, Urban Voodoo: A Beginner's Guide to Afro-Caribbean Magic*
    **Jason Black and Christopher S. Hyatt, Ph.D.**
*The Psychopath's Bible*     **Christopher S. Hyatt, Ph.D., and Jack Willis**
*Ask Baba Lon*     **Lon Milo DuQuette**
*Aleister Crowley and the Treasure House of Images*
    **J.F.C. Fuller, Aleister Crowley, Lon Milo DuQuette and Nancy Wasserman**
*Enochian Sex Magic and How To Workbook*
    **Aleister Crowley, Lon Milo DuQuette and Christopher S. Hyatt, Ph.D.**
*Enochian World of Aleister Crowley*     **DuQuette and Aleister Crowley**
*Info-Psychology, Neuropolitique, The Game of Life, What Does WoMan Want?*
    **Timothy Leary, Ph.D.**
*Paganism in Christian Holidays*     **J. M. Wheeler**
*Lucifer's Rebellion, Reason for Rebellion*     **Compilation**
*Nonlocal Nature: The Eight Circuits of Consciousness*     **James A. Heffernan**
*Numbers Their Meaning and Magic, Vol I, and Vol II, Zodiacal Symbology and It's Planetary Power, Book One and Book Two*     **Isidore Kozminsky**
*on What is*     **Ja Wallin**
*Rebellion, Revolution and Religiousness*     **Osho**
*Reichian Therapy: A Practical Guide for Home Use*     **Dr. Jack Willis**
*Shaping Formless Fire, Seizing Power, Taking Power,*
*The Magick in the Music and Other Essays*     **Stephen Mace**
*The Illuminati Conspiracy: The Sapiens System*     **Donald Holmes, M.D.**
*The Philosophy of Numbers, Vol I and Vol II, Nature's Symphony, Lessons in Number Vibration*     **Mrs. L. Dow Balliett**
*The Secret Inner Order Rituals of the Golden Dawn*     **Pat Zalewski**
*The Why, Who, and What of Existence*     **Vlad Korbel**
*Steamo Goes to Havana, The Social Epidemic of Child Abuse*
    **Michael Miller, M.Ed., M.S., Ph.D.**
*Woman's Orgasm: A Guide to Sexual Satisfaction*
    **Benjamin Graber, M.D., and Georgia Kline-Graber, R.N.**
*Zingara Art of Divinition*     **Ana Calaroni**

**Titles by J. Marvin Spiegelman, Ph.D.**
*A Modern Jew in Search of Soul*
*Buddhism and Jungian Psychology*
*Catholicism and Jungian Psychology*
*Hinduism and Jungian Psychology*
*Mysticism, Psychology and Oedipus - A Small Gem*
*Protestanism and Jungian Psychology*
*Psychotherapy and Religion at the Millennium and Beyond*
*Psychotherapy as a Mutual Process*
*Reich, Jung, Regardie & Me - The Unhealed Healer*
*Rider, Haggard, Henry Miller & I - The Unpublished Writer*
*Sufism, Islam and Jungian Psychology*
*The Knight - A Small Gem*
*The Nymphomaniac*
*The Quest - Further Adventures in the Unconscious*
*The Tree of Life - Paths in Jungian Individuation*
*The Wisdom of J. Marvin Speigelman Vol. I - Selected Writings*
*The Wisdom of J. Marvin Speigelman Vol. II - Psychology and Religion*

## Other Titles by Dr. Israel Regardie
*A Garden of Pomegranates*
*A Practical Guide to Geomantic Divination - A Small Gem*
*Attract and Use Healing Energy - A Small Gem*
*Be Yourself - A Guide to Relaxation and Health*
*Ceremonial Magic*
*Dr. Israel Regardie's Definitive Work on Aleister Crowley,*
  *The Eye In The Triangle*
*Healing Energy, Prayer and Relaxation*
*How To Make and Use Talismans - A Small Gem*
*Israel Regardie's The Foundations of Practical Magick*
*My Rosicrucian Adventure*
*Mysticism, Psychology and Oedipus - A Small Gem*
*Practical Magick - A Small Gem*
*Teachers of Fulfillment*
*The Art and Meaning of Magic - A Small Gem*
*The Body-Mind Connection, A Path to Well-Being - A Small Gem*
*The Complete Golden Dawn System of Magic*
*The Complete Golden Dawn System of Magic Book 1 - Ltd. Edition*
*The Complete Golden Dawn System of Magic Book 2 - Ltd. Edition*
*The Complete Golden Dawn System of Magic - The Black Edition*
*The Eye in the Triangle: An Interpretation of Aleister Crowley*
*The Golden Dawn Audio CDs, Vol. 1, Vol. 2, and Vol. 3*
*The Legend of Aleister Crowley*
*The Magic of Israel Regardie*
*The Middle Pillar*
*The Philosopher's Stone*
*The Portable Complete Golden Dawn System of Magic*
*The Tree of Life*
*The Wisdom of Israel Regardie - Vol. I*
  *Selected Introductions, Prefaces and Forewords*
*The Wisdom of Israel Regardie - Vol. II*
  *Selected Essays and Commentaries*
*The Wisdom of Israel Regardie - Vol. III*
  *Selected Articles, Introductions, Prefaces and Forewords*
*What You Should Know About the Golden Dawn*
*Wilhelm Reich, His Theory And Techniques*
*Aha!* (Dr. Israel Regardie and Aleister Crowley)
*Roll Away The Stone/The Herb Dangerous*
  (Dr. Israel Regardie and Aleister Crowley)

**MANY OF OUR TITLES AVAILABLE ON KINDLE!**
Please visit our website at http://www.newfalcon.com

Copyright ©New Falcon Publications 2024

All rights reserved. No part of this book, in part or in whole, may be reproduced, transmitted, or utilized, in any form or by any means, electronic or mechanical, including photocopying, recording, or by any information storage and retrieval system, without permission in writing from the publisher, except for brief quotations in critical articles, books and reviews.

ISBN 13: 978-156184-053-3
ISBN 10: 1-56184-053-X

New Falcon Publications First Edition 2024

The paper used in this publication meets the minimum requirements
of the American National Standard for Permanence of
Paper for Printed Library Materials Z39.48-1984

Printed in USA

NEW FALCON PUBLICATIONS
2046 Hillhurst Avenue
Los Angeles, CA 90027
www.newfalcon.com
email: info@newfalcon.com

# VOODOO

## AN OUTSIDER'S GUIDE:
### Stories, Spells & Rituals

## S. JASON BLACK

Introduction by Daniel Winston

**NEW FALCON PUBLICATIONS**
LOS ANGELES, CALIFORNIA, U.S.A.

## INTRODUCTION

### By Daniel Winston

It is my welcome task to introduce you to the book "*Voodoo*" by S. Jason Black. Through this book, Black provides us an insider's look at Afro-Caribbean voodoo; a culture to which most people simply do not have access and leads us along the path which first attracted him to the culture and to its practice of this particular form of Magick.

Black was already well acquainted with Magick in other forms having been drawn to it through a series of personal psychic and existential experiences which eventually gave rise to his interest in the practice of the Craft. Black talks frankly about these experiences and how their undeniable presence and influence on him led him to firmly believe in the reality and the power of the metaphysical. Black here is very insistent on Magick being pragmatic and practical. He quite simply, denounces all practices that do not produce actual results; and I mean empirical results. He discusses other practices and groups with which he has sometimes been associated, bravely disputing their worth, with good reason it would seem.

It seems it is in part his search for pure Magickal practice that both honors the ancient craft while never neglecting the need for it to be pertinent and practical in the present day. He takes issue throughout this work with people who practice in a slipshod way, refuting the lies on which some of their practices are based. In this book he captures his struggle to remain true to form, pragmatically separating the wheat from the chaff of Magickal practice itself, hoping to reach the core of truth in it all.

In *Voodoo*, we get the sense that he has found that truth in a craft generally not accessible to an urban white man. Yet he enters that world and lays claim to some of its secrets, without ever having to leave LA. He shares those secrets with us through detailed illustrations and accompanying equally detailed instructions that allow us to perform the rituals and spells of which he speaks. Herein are spells that lead to spirit communion with specific entities he feels are beneficial to the practitioner to entertain and embrace. He calls them by name, discussing their various areas of expertise and domain; along with how to summon them, and exactly what areas of influence they have in the earthly plane.

Black discusses divination at length in its different forms with instructions as to how to create the various devices required or where to find/purchase them. He provides specific illustrations of the accompanying boards required for the various practices.

Later in the book, Black outlines some basic spells. Spells of attraction, luck, money, and several on how to deal with an enemy. He is wise enough to include spells that also handle cleansing and protection. He shares the details of all this as one who speaks from greater experience rather than mere theory for Black is familiar with the broader landscape that includes the psychic, metaphysical, supernatural phenomena, and other forms of Magick in which he has delved.

That is what is so remarkable about this particular book. It is one man's journey driven from within to search for a pure practice which still produces practical results. Everything he shares, he has tried with success in the way of it having produced phenomena. His perspective is one from the mystical trenches rather than a bystander merely reporting, attempting to appear casually unbiased. And his perspective serves him; bringing him into a sometimes-darker realm which he in the end transcends to our benefit. Archetypally this work is a little bit of a hero's journey. At least a hero's exploration. And it is the personal aspect of this that draws us in. Black is by no means cute and cuddly, and some of his views may seem a little extreme but what we cannot take away in the end is the sense that underneath it all there lies a sensitive, man of honor who deserves our respect and admiration. And I give that to him here. Black was sometimes misunderstood in life, but here we have a tribute to him and his exploration into the metaphysical that I feel exonerates him in the end.

*Downtown Los Angeles Botanica*

# PREFACE

# HOODOO WAR
### S. Jason Black

About a year ago I was leaving the Grand Central Market in downtown Los Angeles. It was a rainy afternoon, and I was carrying about a zillion bags of groceries, so the moment I was outside I huddled against the wall away from the street as best I could. The Grand Central Market is an enormous enclosed space that covers a city block and is more or less the equivalent of a "farmers market." The fresh vegetables and baked goods are incredibly cheap so I made a habit of visiting it about once a month to stock up my freezer.

For the last twenty years or so, this particular section of downtown has become increasingly occupied by shops and markets owned by, or aimed at, the enormous Latino population of the area. These include not only Mexican residents, but an ever-increasing presence of immigrants from Central and South America and from Cuba. If you hit the area on a Saturday or Sunday Afternoon, you get the distinct feeling of being in some Brazilian marketplace.

At any rate, here am I, huddled against the wall by the corner trying to stay dry. Having my hands full, and with nothing better to do, I turn and look at the display window of the drug store I was leaning against. My eyes stray across cold remedies, mouthwash, tampons, Voodoo dolls...

Voodoo dolls?

I haul myself and my zucchini into the store.

The place that I walked into is called the Million Dollar Pharmacy, and is on the corner of Broadway and Third. I suppose that it is indeed a pharmacy, and it is certainly a drugstore in the ordinary sense, but mostly it is something quite different.

Fully a third to a half of the store is taken up by what is politely referred to as "religious goods." In other words, what was a pharmacy on the outside, was, on the inside, a Botanica–a supply shop for the practice of Voodoo and Brujeria.

There were racks of bagged dried herbs, candles in various recherché forms and tiny little talismans made from stamped metal, some of which I recognized, many of which I did not. There were floor washes and bath soaps to attract money or to destroy evil influence, good cigars for ritual use, racks of booklets in Spanish or Portuguese containing spells and incantations, and endearing little statues of Eleggua (more on him later) for home or office.

On the other side of the room were many seemingly orthodox items. There were crucifixes of various sizes in the baroque Catholic style, one or two rosaries and a glass case containing beautiful little statues of various saints. I already knew my subject, however, so I wasn't fooled by this show of Christian piety. The saints were all the "masks" of the various daemons of Afro-Caribbean magic, used as talismans and altarpieces by practitioners who don't want the local priest–or members of their family–to know what they are really into.

Below these were some striking items that I had never seen before. They were pyramid-shaped objects of cast Lucite containing carefully arranged cultic and talismanic objects that gave effect of sculptures suspended in colored air. These were obviously hand made and, upon study, I realized that they were talismans, each made for a specific purpose, such as money attraction. These seemed to be magical items, intended to be thought of as paperweights by the uninitiated. In much the same vein, they were Chinese Buddhas with similar magic symbols cast into them–another mask.

I walked out without buying anything–that time. While I was startled to have discovered that little wonderland in such an accidental way, especially after passing it a hundred times before, I wasn't all that surprised. Traveling between downtown and Hollywood–where I was living at the time–I could count around ten botanicas just on Sunset Boulevard as it led through the Boyle

Heights district and Silverlake into Hollywood proper. In Los Angeles, as in cities like New York and Miami, businesses catering to *Santeria* and the various other Voodoo religions outnumber not only "occult" shops, but *Christian book stores* about five to one.

The weird thing about this is that, except for sociologist and "cult experts," no one outside the religions themselves *even know they exist*. This includes people who live cheek by jowl with these shops, and individuals, such as big city journalists, who should know better.

Example: A couple of years ago, I was watching the local evening news and the local anchorman appeared with a great big inverted pentagram blue screened behind him. "Oh boy!" I thought, "Here comes some fun." There followed a report of what the newsman and the police both referred to as "Satanic rituals" being performed in the San Pedro area (a district near Los Angeles harbor with a large Hispanic population). The evidence for this included a rather sizable number of slaughtered chickens and maybe a goat or two in a dumpster. I was shocked. Not because of the alleged sacrifice of things people eat for lunch, but because they and the candles discovered along with them were obviously the remains of a *Santeria* celebration. Any magic that was involved was probably white as the driven snow. Yet, both our beloved Los Angeles Police Department and the professional journalists, both of whom should know better, never used the word but Satanism throughout the report. This in reference to a religion that I would guess conservatively to be half a million strong in Los Angeles county and with a much richer history.

My outrage at this demonstration of bigoted Christian ignorance was certainly in the minority, if not unique. Most of the W.A.S.P. population certainly didn't question the identification of this "outrage" (give me a break) as Satanism. In the Christian population, even in Los Angeles, the christening (sorry) of anything non-Christian as Satanism is a given. To a large extent this is also true among people with no particular religious affiliation or interest. Only a few people of European extraction are even aware of *Santeria* and its kin, much less sympathetic to it as I am.

Let me make myself clear. I have absolutely nothing against Satanism. I made it clear in a previous book *Pacts With the Devil*, New Falcon Publications, 1993, that it is a perfectly valid system of self-development and liberation along with the other forms of Goetic occultism handed down from European ancestors. I *am* offended by the cowardly and emotionally crippling form of "Neo-Paganism" that today claims to be witchcraft.

What horrifies me is the use of the term as a weapon against a religious tradition who's roots were old when the myth of Moses was just being formulated.

There are comparatively few books in English on the Voodoo phenomenon from the point of view of the practitioner and most have been in print in one form or another for many years–the excellent and encyclopedic works of Migene Gonzalez-Wippler and Maya Deren, for example. Almost without exception, these books, including Ms. Wippler's, tend to whitewash certain aspects of the Voodoo magician's relationship to the world around him and attempts to make it palatable and acceptable to Christian society.

I have no such intention.

To begin with, I know first-hand the futility of attempting to appease a fascist religious philosophy whose stated purpose for the last millennium has been the elimination of all other religions of the world. Over the course of time, this campaign of destruction has been expanded to include scholars, homosexuals, women, children, artists, and anyone displaying any talent in the area of human psychic functioning. This leaves a narrow spectrum of humanity–who are acceptable in the eyes of "God."

That vision of ultra-conservative loveliness, Pat Buchanan, has said that we are in the midst of a "cultural civil war." *I agree.*

Western culture in general, and the United States in particular, are in a situation that has struck Umberto Ecco as curiously similar to the Middle Ages. By this I mean that there are currently two or more distinct cultures, cultures with different goals, lifestyles, and religions that are *incapable of coexisting without violence.*

Please understand, I am not referring to some "racial problem." I am referring to the attack by what is known as "Christian Right" on the civil rights–if not the very existence–of certain groups of people who will no longer submit to psychological disfigurement.

What has this to do with Voodoo? Simply this: of all the techniques of self-empowerment in history, there is practically only one that has survived the Inquisitorial onslaught and remained essentially intact and in harmony with its prehistoric roots: Voodoo.

Ripped by war and the slave trade from its ancient shores, it developed as a form of occult guerrilla warfare against a religio-military plague that spread across the planet. What I refer to as the "Voodoo religions:– Haitian Voodoo, *Santeria*, and *Macumba*–are now collectively one of the largest religions in the world.

And yet, in this country at least, almost no one has heard of it. In fact, on a recent episode of "The McLaughlin Group" there was a commentary on the perennial troubles in Haiti. In a brief prologue they gave some statistics on the island nation. Among other things it was referred to as simply 80% Catholic.

This ridiculous lapse on a national news program (on which the lovely Pat Buchanan used to appear) was obviously due to Christian bigotry, pure and simple. Whoever had prepared the statistical segment couldn't bring themselves to call Voodoo a religion on television.

It is due both to this form of censorship and its own commitment to secrecy that Voodoo remains invisible to the population at large (in America at any rate).

I am talking about a secret society of sorcerers, with traditions old enough and numbers large enough to challenge the Judeo-Christian tyranny. This makes many of the segments of the "New Age" movement–whether I talk about followers of Crowley or so-called "Wiccans"– look irrelevant, something that the next several decades may ultimately prove them to be. They are, taken together, only a few thousand strong. Large enough to be noted and prosecuted, but not large enough to fight back. Nor, from my own extensive experience of these movements, are any of these people even remotely interested in the practice of magic, only in the practice of self-deception.

On the other hand, as I write this, an Afro-Caribbean religious group in Florida has brought their right to the religious sacrifice of animals before the Supreme Court of the United States–and won. It should be noted, as an aside, that at no time did the Jews have to appeal to the Supreme Court for permission to have a rabbi cut the throat of a chicken or cow and offer the blood to Jehovah. This, for those of you who don't know, is know kosher meats are made. So every time you bite into a Hebrew National hot dog, you are partaking in part of a blood sacrifice. What an outrage! Call the police!

Since the Christian Right has declared war, this book is intended, in part at least, as a tool of guerrilla warfare.

Where the Judeo-Christian religions and most of the New Age movement tell you to repress your emotions and desires and to (pretend to) think "happy thoughts",

I say, along with the ancient Voodoo gods, that desire is honorable, that anger may well be justified, that the will to power is nothing to be ashamed of.

This book partly tells the story of my involvement in the traditions of Voodoo and how it came about. These are stories to be told about "religious experiences" and "psychic phenomena", but each of these has, as its ultimate objective, "getting things done."

This book will not tell you that lust is "unspiritual" or that a money spell is "low magic." Nor will I tell you that curses are forbidden and will "rebound on the sender." All of this is rubbish promoted by failures who use the trappings of "spirituality" as a sop for their own inferiority; thus to them, lack of success, in a dizzying reversal, becomes proof of spiritual advancement.

The Voodoo gods are in the world, and to them the world is good, and so are the desires the world produces.

Many of the books I have read on Voodoo have, in a well-meaning, but pompous fashion, insisted that these practices should not be undertaken without initiation. I flatly deny this. This book is written from the point of view not of the *Houngan*–the community priest–but of the *Bocar*–the sorcerer. It is for the outsider raised in another tradition who may never see a *Santeria* priest in his life. It is for the lone practitioner, or the small group.

It is for guerrilla spiritual warfare against fascist religions that want you under their heels.

But especially, it's for getting things done.

I want to bring real magic, the genuine experience of the psychic and the supernatural, to the aspirant in the modern world. Here there is no need to dress in costumes from the covers of fantasy novels, or to try to "worship" deities fabricated by a potty old Englishman after World War II.

If you call, according to the formulae handed down from antiquity, I can assure you from my own experience when something answers you will not be able to write it off as "creative imagination" or "the experience of an archetype."

The magic works, and blends as nicely now, in the information age, as it did in the time of the schooner.

Maybe better.

# CONTENTS

| | | |
|---|---|---|
| Introduction by Daniel Winston | | vii |
| Preface by S. Jason Black | | xi |
| *Chapter 1* | **Initiation** | 1 |
| *Chapter 2* | **White Zombie** | 15 |
| *Chapter 3* | **The Gods Are Angry Effendi** | 27 |
| *Chapter 4* | **Tell My Horses–Go Back to Missouri** | 33 |
| *Chapter 5* | **Dead Men Work in the Fields of Hollywood** | 39 |
| *Chapter 6* | **Spirits That Findeth Hidden Treasure** | 51 |
| *Chapter 7* | **Divination Techniques** | 63 |
| *Chapter 8* | **The Lords of the Crossroads** | 89 |
| *Chapter 9* | **Some Other Members of the Family** | 105 |
| *Chapter 10* | **Cocaine, Zombies & Cauldrons of Blood** | 117 |
| *Chapter 11* | **Spells** | 125 |
| *Chapter 12* | **Initiation & Self-Initiation** | 133 |

*The Long Beach Freeway*

## Chapter 1
# INITIATION

I used to think that my "conversion" to the alien world view of another time and culture was unique. I am, you see, of Scotch Irish ancestry and was raised in the Midwest. I was later to find that it was not unique at all, but almost stereotypical. It involved a series of weird experiences that bordered on (and sometimes leapt over the border of) the supernatural. After years of reading, I found that not only had a number of other European immigrants had very similar experiences, but the process was nearly traditional. Especially in Haiti and Brazil, people are often "selected" by the spirits rather than the other way around.

My "conversion" didn't come completely out of the blue. I had been involved in the serious practice of magic for a large portion of my life, the interest triggered by psychic experiences I had had since I was small. I emphasize *serious* practice. By this I mean things intended to produce tangible results or observable phenomena, such as the prediction of the future or the conjuration of spirits. These activities produced startling results with great regularity, or I would have given up the practice. By magic I definitely do *not* mean 'Gnostic Masses" or "Drawing Down The Moon" or any other "religious" ritual that calls itself magic. These rituals may have some magical overtones but they are not the magic that I am speaking of.

First, a little prologue, to give some idea of the kinds of phenomena that I had experienced on a fairly routine basis:

About nine years ago I was residing in the city of Long Beach, a few miles south of Los Angeles. I was intensely bored with the place, and wanted to move north to the Hollywood area. To facilitate this I had taken a job in the Wilshire business district of Los Angeles, which meant an exhausting daily commute. Almost all I did was work and sleep, which kept me in a constant state of exhaustion. I tell you this to give some idea of my long-term physical and emotional state at the time–which has a great deal to do with the story.

I was working in a large office, dealing with crates of legal documents that had to be gone over and itemized for a corporate lawsuit, so as you can guess, the work was boring as well. Many of you have experienced the behavior that long-term boredom produces in an office. I am not referring to good-natured tomfoolery.

Among my coworkers was a rather "Junoesque" (i.e., clinically obese) black woman who sat at the desk next to me. She put on a great show of being jovial and good-natured for the (absentee) supervisor, and then did whatever the hell she wanted to the rest of the time. The result of this tactic is that if a complaint is filed, the complainer is not believed, and furthermore, labeled a troublemaker. I had already seen this, and so chose to remain silent when I became her target.

She was not my superior in the office hierarchy–it wasn't that kind of abusive behavior. It was the kind of thing that starts out as a few jokes at your expense and then escalates to open insults said deliberately within your hearing.

This woman's appetite for this kind of thing was greater than any I have since encountered. I had seen her do this to others, who, like myself, had hardly every spoken to her, much less done anything to her.

This ordeal went on hour after hour, day after day, until, for one of the very few times in my life, I seriously considered physical violence. I was actually trying to calculated how much jail time I would get with no previous record if I disfigured her with a staple remover.

One day I nearly did it. I was so tired and her behavior was so vicious, that it literally took all my willpower not to attack her physically. For a few seconds my blood pressure was so high that, for the first time, I literally saw red.

During the long, slow ride home, part of my mind seemed to detach itself and go its own way without my volition. While still seeing what was around me, I was also watching a surreal little movie in my head, the images of which I quite literally had no control over.

In it, I saw a pair of hands (mine?) molding what appeared a soft black wax into the lumpy form of what the woman at work would look like if I had the misfortune to see her naked. When this work was done, the hands took a box of pins and stuck them in the figure's stomach until it looked like a pincushion. Then I came back to myself. Except for some strange bodily sensations that accompanied this, and the bizarre sense that I was watching a movie that I could not control, I more or less dismissed the experience as idle imagination stimulated by anger and exhaustion.

I arrived home and, as usual, was in bed within an hour.

My eyes opened in the small hours of the morning. The luminous dial on my watch told me it was three a.m. I had awakened with the *sure knowledge* that something was going to happen to that woman during the next work day.

I had to get up at 5:30 a.m., so I returned to sleep as quickly as I could.

When the alarm went off before dawn, I could hardly move because of the interruption in my rest, but move I did. When I went out into the hall, I had a strange sense of foreboding. When I put my hand on the light switch to the living room, I froze. I stared into the living room darkness with the feeling that something was there, and that something was about to happen. I flipped the switch, and the bulb in the living room *exploded*. Not *popped*, like an ordinary bulb that burns out, but exploded into pieces. I could find nothing wrong with the lamp or the wiring. So, "big deal," you're thinking, right?

I dragged my hollow self to Los Angeles and then to work.

With bags under my eyes large enough for a winter wardrobe, I sit at my desk. SHE comes in and sits at the desk next to me. We work. Suddenly, I'm disturbed by a sharp cry of pain to my left. My evil genius has her chair pushed back, her eyes squeezed shut and her hands clutching her stomach.

Someone (not me) asks if she is OK. She complains of sharp pain in her stomach. They suggest she go lie down and she complies.

After half an hour, the pains have not subsided, and she goes home, not to return until the end of the following week. The story she told was this: the pains increased in intensity so she called her family doctor for an emergency appointment. His verdict was that he had no idea what was going on, and made arrangements for her to be checked into the hospital the same day. The hospital staff–according to her account–examined her, X-rayed her, and kept her under observation for three days until the pain passed, again, unable to find a cause.

Within two weeks of her return, she departed my office for a job at the post office.

Besides being an explanation of some of the problems of the U.S. Postal Service, this is one of the finest examples of "primitive" sympathetic magic that I have ever experienced. Except for the location in Los Angeles, and the fact that the doll was in my mind and not physical reality, this story could have come from one of those "Ju-Ju in my life" books British explorers used to write.

Two more first-hand accounts before the story of how I became involved in Afro-Caribbean magic, both classic: the love charm and the protective charm. Bear in mind that, as I tell these stories, I have deliberately chosen examples that had an *affect on the physical world*. I want to emphasize that I am not talking about "positive thinking" or "creative visualization," but something else that our culture does not accept. Bear in mind also, that whatever impression the following narrative may give, I have not spent the last fifteen years of my life attempting to curse or bend people to my will. This, as I will make clear, is a great deal of work. But such stories make the best examples by their very nature. Tales of "supernatural advancement" often sound like, and often are, cases for the psych ward rather than theology.

Some years before I decided to move to Hollywoodland, I hung around with, and experimented magically with a young woman who was one of the best mediums I had ever encountered. She was a bass player/legal typist who could type 120 words per minute with no mistakes and was frequently wacky as a jay bird.

She was also an aspiring poet with a sound knowledge of the Los Angeles underground scene. We had already done a lot of weird things together when she came to me with a kind of archetypal request, but one that I had never done on another person's behalf before. It turned out the side-effects were more interesting than the results.

She was one of those people who change boyfriends like some people change automobiles. And she was usually shopping for the next one while still attached to the first. So it was no great surprise when she told me she had just met someone that she already considered herself in love with. He was temperamentally rather conservative–hardly her usual type–so she couldn't just ask him for a vow of undying devotion, or make one herself, especially since she had only known him less than a week.

Since we had performed a few occult experiments that gave the appearance of producing results, she asked me if I would make a love talisman for her. I said that I would be glad to, but I had no way of obtaining a magical link with a man that I didn't know. That was no problem, she said, and produced from her purse a used condom that she waved blithely in front of my face.

After convincing her to please put the thing down, she also produced a carefully drawn love talisman from the *Key of Solomon*.

I laid out the necessary equipment (pentacles, incense, etc.) and then we laid down a magic circle of protection.

For the most part the talismans described in the *Key of Solomon* are intended to attract a certain *class* of spirit rather than a specific angel or demon. Since this was the method she had chosen, I followed along in the correct manner according to the book and called on a venereal spirit in the name of several supposed higher intelligences. I instructed it to appear to the woman, and to compel her new paramour to commit himself to her in an unambiguous way. We spent some time in an auto-hypnotic state, willing the appropriate intelligence to hear the request and to manifest itself in the physical world.

Several days later, she phoned. She said that the object of her lust had intensified his attentions to her since the day after the conjuration and had asked her to move in with him. Apparently he had interspersed all of this with comments on his confusion at being so strongly attracted to someone normally not his type.

All of this can be dismissed, as with so many spells that "work," as something that was going to happen anyway, rather like the Egyptian priests commanding the Nile to rise in its season of flooding. I wasn't made aware of the really interesting part until she came by to visit the following weekend.

I asked her if there had been any "signs and wonders" of any sort following our ceremony, and, frowning, she said she thought there had been. She had had an intense hypnogogic experience while lying in bed that interesting state between sleeping and waking.

She had, she claimed, been visited by "monsters" that had tried to communicate with her, but had only been able to do so in a kind of pantomime. She described them as the sort of impossible mixture of species that one finds in ancient mythologies. At first I didn't see any connection between this experience and what we had done. Any old dream didn't become a psychic experience just because it followed on the heels of an act of ritual magic. However, something was nagging in the back of my mind when she described what seemed to be the principle beast that wanted to attract her attention. I asked her to draw a picture of it.

She made a quick sketch and a chill went down my spine. I went to my art portfolio, pulled something out, and showed it to her.

"Did it look like this?" I asked.

She got a shocked look on her face. "Yes!" She said, "That's it!"

What I had pulled out of storage was a painting I had done some years before, of a vision I had had during the evocation of a demon from the demonology called the "*Goetia*." The painting that I had done in no way matches the traditional description in the book itself and my friend had never, ever seen it. In point of fact, I hadn't even thought of it for quite some time, as the operation had had some rather frightening and unrequested results. We include both pictures here so that you may judge for yourself.

*Female Medium's drawing and author's painting of spirit Beleth*

Here is the description of the demon and its offices from the *Goetia*:

The thirteenth spirit is called Beleth. He is a terrible and mighty King. He rides upon a pale horse. Trumpets and other kinds of musical instruments play before him. He is very furious at his first appearance, that is, while the Exorcist lays his courage... This Great King Beleth causes all the love that may be, both of men and of women, until the Master exorcist has had his desire fulfilled. He is of the order of powers... etc., etc.

We took this little trick to be the communication of the spirit's presence that we had originally requested. It is not to be taken as proof that Beleth "really" exists–in the form of a King of Hell at any rate.

The argument over the existence or nonexistence of spirits will be taken up later in this book.

The "protection" story took place a few years earlier. I had not been long in Southern California from the

Midwest, and was taking graduate courses at the local branch of the California University system. To support that activity I worked as a driver for a state-sponsored food program, similar to "meals on wheels." It operated out of the University food service so that I could work without destroying my school schedule.

The manager of the program was–to be polite–a highly strung woman that I almost never had to see. To make a long story short, I began to receive written "warnings" from her about work events that *never occurred!*

Or, when they had, they had happened to someone else. I quietly pointed this out to a supervisor beneath her in her office. The response I received (confidentially of course) was: "Oh, she's had a fight with her ex-husband. You'd better start sending out resumes." This did not seem responsive so I asked for an explanation.

I was told that she periodically had great rows with her ex-husband, who was one of my professors at the University. When this occurred, she routinely picked someone to fire in order to make herself feel better, and this time I was it.

I could not afford to accept this fate as it would essentially wreck my schedule of graduate work and, besides, (goddammit!), it was completely unjustified. Of course, that was irrelevant.

At that time I was already heavily involved in experimentation with occult material supposedly given to the Elizabethan mathematician Dr. John Dee by "angels."

Of course, one must keep in mind that what a Renaissance religious theoretician means by angels is not what the average lay person means by the same word. During a successful conjuration–more of a seance really–I had had a clairvoyant vision which included a talisman to be made of raw clay, and instructions for its use (the details of this will be related later.)

According to the instructions I received, I fashioned the talisman from wet potter's clay and allowed it to dry. Then, early one morning before work, I placed it underneath the outdoor stairs leading to this woman's pre-fab office unit–the only way in or out. This–some of you will recognize–is typical of witchcraft techniques from every culture.

The result? After more than a decade at that job she quit, unexpectedly, and with only a week's notice. This occurred about three weeks after I planted the talisman, and only a few days before the first rain of the season dissolved it into nothing.

This story, I will be the first to admit, is far more circumstantial than the first two, and could easily be called "coincidence." However, there are two similar stories that I will relate later which are more striking.

All three of these event took place years before my experiences with "Voodoo" began, but they are excellent examples of the sort of phenomena that occur during the serious practice of magic. In fact, I would say that this sort of thing is "par for the course" if you take the trouble to do the work and follow instructions–instructions which tend to be almost identical in magical texts and traditions from all parts of the world. The principle differences between Voodoo and the so-called "Western Tradition" is that, in spite of the travails of history, Afro-Caribbean magic remained essentially intact in technique. The European material has been heavily censored and bowdlerized by its (principally Victorian) editors, with bogus notions of "karma" and other delusions about divine retribution culled principally from Theosophy and the Church. In no traditional magical system–oriental or occidental–does this nonsense exist in the original material. It is the self-defensive fantasy of a frightened middle-class mid-zonal mentality.

When I refer to "traditional" magical or esoteric systems I want the reader to understand that I am not referring to Wicca or the so-called Neo-Pagan movements, which tend to be largely based on bogus history or even (see Gerald Gardner) outright fraud.

*The Bodhi Tree Bookstore in West Hollywood*

*Chapter 2*

# WHITE ZOMBIE

My experiences with Voodoo began about 1983 or 1984. I had been involved with the "occult" for many years and had been in, or on the fringes of, a number of organized groups, particularly one based on the writings of Aleister Crowley. Out of frustration, I began to withdraw from these associations. I had come to the growing, and disappointing, realization that while most so-called "magical orders" claimed to teach and practice magic, almost none of them did so. I must say, in justice, that for a period of more than two years, there was a core group who would drive long distances up to twice a week to spend hours in serious experiments. We worked with the "Enochian system" produced by Dr. John Dee in the sixteenth century. This work produced tangible results including "speaking in tongues," repeated poltergeist phenomena during some of the seances and the successful casting of "spells" using talismans clairvoyantly received.

Sadly, in time this practice stopped. What remained were the rote repetition of "classes" to new members, and the endless repetition of religious rituals, especially Crowley's "Gnostic Mass." With the death of the first organization's head in the U.S. the encouragement of many experimental practices decreased. Some members have declared the Gnostic Mass to be the "central ritual" of the order–whatever that means–and gradually some members came to believe that if you practiced the mass you were practicing magic. There are a few remarks by Crowley used to justify this, but it is clear from his overall writings that he never intended his occult training system to consist primarily of the Gnostic Mass.

All I can say is, that if *just* performing Crowley's mass makes you a magician, then every Episcopal or Presbyterian minister in the world is a magus.

And they ain't.

For those of you unfamiliar with it, the Gnostic Mass was written by Crowley as the communion ritual for his projected new religion of "Crowleyanity." It was based on the Episcopal high mass, with the Christian elements replaced with pagan ones and a tiny touch of the Black Mass thrown in for good measure. In places it is quite beautiful. In others it retains the tedium of the original.

The capper on my frustration came when, several years ago, I attended a performance of one of the "Rites of Eleusis" in the hills in California. These Rites are from Crowley's early attempts to recreate the ceremonies of classical paganism. When it was over I was sitting at a table with several people in casual conversation about the "Crowley's group" and other topics. I don't remember how it came up, but I recall expressing my disturbance at the apparent lack of experience by "initiates" of some years standing in occult practice of *any* kind, even in something as basic as yoga. I described some of my own experiences and I was told that no one had ever experienced anything like that. I then asked if anyone present had ever executed a ceremony of ritual magic. After a few moments of dead air, one man said that he had once done the Gnostic Mass. When I pointed out to him that that was more a *religious ritual*, he said "Oh. I was told it was magic."

That was pretty much the end–for a number of years– of my involvement with Crowley's group, although not with his writings and philosophy.

The point of all of this is simply that I had come to a personal dead end. As someone who had spent enormous time and energy exploring the processes of Western magic (by which I mean *practicing* it) this development filled me with disgust. It also pointed out to me a phenomenon I have seen repeatedly: the white European/ Christian fear of the supernatural. The vast majority of "occult orders" that I have come into contact with have found some way to avoid the very experiences for which they are supposed to exist. In recent years I have come to call these people "church ladies" since they pretend to be something that they are not and create a fantasy world of identification and comfort just like any of the Christian cults. (In contradistinction to many Crowley and Golden Dawn groups, Chaos Magick seems to hold hope for the serious student).

The result was that, probably like the majority of people involved in esoteric disciplines, I began to practice alone or with a few select partners.

I have had psychic experiences since I was quite small. In fact, the inability of my Presbyterian minister or Sunday school teachers to answer my questions about these (Presbyterianism is radically non-mystical) was what started my interest in the occult. During the intervening years I had become adept a tarot card divination, astrology, pendulum dowsing, and trance work. I spent a brief period as a professional psychic and a much longer period giving readings for businesses (something I still do.)

I mention this to make it clear to the reader that when the events I am about to describe began, I was not in the least a novice. I would also like to repeat that, at the time, I had no interest in Voodoo whatsoever. What little I had read about it rather turned me off.

I was sensing an impending change. I was working at a job in the broadcasting industry for which I had had high hopes. Unfortunately the business situation was going downhill, not just for me, but for people all over the company. Promised promotions did not take place, there was nasty in-fighting, the economy sucked (it was the Reagan Prosperity Period) and one executive who had just been moved from the east coast had resigned–"or something." No one was sure, it was that kind of atmosphere.

One night in the midst of this, I performed a ritual to cleanse the atmosphere, a basic pentagram ritual. (See *The Complete Golden Dawn System of Magic*, New Falcon Publications, 2022) and performed an evocation of what I considered to be a "familiar spirit" called Orox.

I used a professionally made and balanced dowser's pendulum for basic communication during this exercise. The pendulum gives positive/negative answers as well as measuring degrees of "intensity" regarding the subject inquired about.

I was informed that I had better be prepared for a move, since the situation I was in was unstable (big revelation–I already knew this). Furthermore, I was to get in touch with another energy–or order of beings, it was unclear–and what's more *they* were calling *me*. All of this was the result of an hour or more of probing with the pendulum, a process that was more than a little tedious.

For those of you who have no previous experience of this subject–either personally or through reading–this must already sound fishy. "Oh, right. They were *calling* him." For those of you with some knowledge of shamanic religious experience, this must sound familiar.

After the tedious process of getting this "revelation" I proceeded with the tedious process of finding out what the hell it meant. (People who pursue the occult for "the thrill" always tickle my funny bone.)

This was a simple process of elimination. Since I was dealing with a yes/no oracle, I needed a word or sentence to work from. I asked if a reference to what I was seeking existed in my personal library.

"Yes."

Was the reference in a fiction or non-fiction book?

"Non-fiction."

I then began, one by one, to name the reference books on my shelves until the pendulum indicated I had named the correct one. It was *Cults of The Shadow* by British author Kenneth Grant.

I opened the table of contents and went through the same process until I was told what chapter to look in, and repeated it again with the page number and then the paragraph.

Some of you may be thinking that the subject I was "directed to" should have been obvious to me once the book was selected. If so, you have not read the works of the fabulous Mr. Grant. Most of the later ones, including *Cults of The Shadow*, give the impression of being written in a state of frenzied delirium, with subjects that don't connect from paragraph to paragraph, and historical "facts" that he seemed to fabricate on the spot. In many places it is such a word-salad that the oracle could have been directing me to almost any subject in the world.

As it was, it turned out to be something I would have to go out to research anyway.

The word–and the whole answer was reduced to something that small and specific–was *Ifa*, a *Yoruba* deity name that is mentioned only briefly in an early chapter of Grant's book. Mr. Grant claimed that this was the name of the "African Venus." What's more, I can say with absolute certainty that *Ifa* was mentioned in no other book I owned at the time.

"*Yorubas?*" I thought, "*Ifa?*" I thought, "For god's sake, *Venus?*" What has this to do with my problems?

I asked the pendulum if this was correct. It insisted, repeatedly, that it was. Having no reference that I could study, beyond Grant's few sentences that made no sense, I gave up on it for the night and went to bed.

The following evening after work I went to the Bodhi Tree bookstore in West Hollywood, one of the largest religious/occult bookstores in the country. I went there instead of the public library, having learned from repeated experience that if the library had ever had good references to a subject like Voodoo, they had already been stolen. Also I felt I might want to own my source of information.

Unfortunately, the selection of books on African religion or Voodoo were rather small that night, and what there was, was related to Haitian Voodoo, which is Dahomean not *Yoruban* (though there are many connections) with no references to poor old *Ifa*, whoever she was. I gave up in disgust and began browsing at random, putting the matter out of my mind. After a little while I picked up a (then) new book called *The Oracle of Geomancy* by Stephen Skinner.

For those of you not familiar with Geomancy, it is a rather complex form of divination which combines some of the symbols and forms of astrology with ancient "earth" magic. It was extensively used by Renaissance magi like Agrippa, and was part of the Golden Dawn curriculum. Dr. Israel Regardie used Geomantic Divination extensively and wrote a small gem named *A Practical Guide to Geomantic Divination* published by New Falcon Publications, 2018.

While glancing at the introduction to the book, to my utter amazement I saw a complete description of the history of *Ifa!* *Ifa* was male, not female, and had nothing whatever to do with Venus. *Ifa* was a sort of "elder god" who had given both the gods and men the art of divination and then went about his business rather like the Greek Titans. He was also intimately involved with luck and with the performance of miracles. This was completely in line with my personal needs.

Except for the name, everything in the Kenneth Grant book was totally incorrect.

I emphasize this to point out the fact that not only had I no previous interest in this *Ifa*, but the only reference I had in my possession was utterly erroneous. This makes it less likely that my guidance to this subject "sprouted from my unconscious."

A couple of evenings later, I performed a conjuration of "Ifa" using what little information I had. In European magic, as well as its Voodoo cousins, a "link" is usually formed with the spirit to be conjured using either a symbol or icon traditionally associated with it. (Full instructions will be given later in this book. Also see *Pacts With the Devil* (1993) and *Aleister Crowley's Illustrated Goetia* (1992) both from New Falcon Publications). I had none of these traditional tools to work with, so I simply asked for some sort of "sign." I have done this before with some success, frequently receiving lucid dreams or weird synchronicities in response.

In this case, I began having dreams of floating figures that spoke to me, and exotic tropical landscapes I didn't recognize. Again, these were only dreams, and I don't present them as psychic phenomena, but they were noticeable as something unusual, and continued night after night for about a week.

I had purchased a book with some Voodoo material in it, but it referenced only Haitian Voodoo, and *Ifa* was not mentioned in that pantheon of spirits. This was another rather odd thing about the experience. What little I had ever read about Voodoo had been about Haiti. The tradition I was trying to find out about was, to my personal experience, utterly obscure. This further indicated that these "omens" were not cobbled together from my previous knowledge. It was soon to be driven home to me just how very little I knew about a world of magic that existed all around me.

I continued to perform my crude conjurations and tried to research my subject during the evening and while dealing with an increasingly chaotic office during the day. The only tangible results of my efforts seemed to be an increasing feeling of eeriness and tension, as though something were about to happen. Sometimes I had the feeling of being followed, which made me feel neither secure nor particularly sane.

The first certainty that I was having what the *hoi poloi* would call a "religious experience," and what I prefer to think of in paranormal terms, came on the third weekend after I began my magical experimentation. I was walking home alone quite late one night. I had just seen a movie at a local art house. For those who know Hollywood, I was on Franklin Avenue walking west from Vermont. This is an old residential area that was quite popular with movie people in the 1920s and still contains some impressive and well-maintained property. I wasn't nervous; I knew the area very well–I lived there–and there wasn't a potential mugger in sight. Just me and the skunks from Griffith Park. My mind was totally involved with the conjurations that I had been performing on almost a nightly basis, and I had decided that since–except for the dreams, which were not convincing enough–I had not received the requested "sign", I would drop the whole matter.

At the moment that I made that decision, I felt a crawling sensation along my skin, and the streetlights around me went out.

I stopped.

Telling myself to please not be a fool, I continued my walk, but the weird crawling sensation remained present. To calm myself down and also to test the situation, I said out loud, "If this is a spirit manifestation, then do it again." By this time I was two or three blocks away from the light failure and all the streetlights were normal.

The moment I spoke those words, the lights on my block, and *only* on my block, went out.

This, to my mind, was starting to push coincidence, and my walk home became much speedier. By the time I reached the lobby of my apartment building I started to dismiss it again–after all, streetlights went out in Los Angeles all the time. I stood waiting for the elevator to take me to my apartment and, when it appeared, since I still had the feeling of a "presence" I just said "OK, if you're there, do it again."

At that moment the elevator lights went out, and the elevator door began shuddering open and shut like a spastic colon.

I ran, did not walk, up the stairs to my home.

As an interesting aside nearly a year after the first draft of this book was written an article appeared in the Long Beach Press Telegram regarding a man who grew up in Beverly Hills and was told by several black musician friends that spirits were calling him. According to his story when he resisted this since it was alien to his background street lights would go out whenever he walked down the streets at night and this continued until he gave in and went to Africa to be initiated as a spirit medium. This man was also white.

*Chapter 3*

# THE GODS ARE ANGRY EFFENDI

By this time I became a little disturbed.

It wasn't that I hadn't experienced this sort of thing before–I had. If the practice of ceremonial magic hadn't produced this sort of result for me I would have lost interest years before (some of these events are related in an earlier book *Pacts With The Devil*, New Falcon Publications, 1993). Nonetheless, interference with the city electrical system was new to me.

I continued to have frequent feelings of being followed or watched, as well as that odd crawling sensation on my skin. These feelings, incidentally, seem to be identical with the "vibrations" described by American and European esotericism, and had practiced yoga and other trance-inducing techniques, I felt increasingly that I didn't know what to expect from what I had "called up." Because of my years of study, I have rarely needed outside advice to deal with psychic or occult phenomena, but now found myself casting around for some sort of knowledgeable human resource. I found it closer to home than I expected, in the form of an occult supply shop that was almost an institution in the area–the "House of Hermetic."

This was a nondescript (on the outside) but sizable store that catered to the occult and witchcraft community in the Hollywood area with books, candles, fresh herbs and hand-blended incenses. I sought out one of the owners of the place and told him what had been happening to me. I didn't go into detail, but I did mention that I had experienced what may have been "poltergeist phenomena." He had no problem with the story at all and implied that he had heard that sort of thing before. As well as Wicca and related practices, the store also catered to the local *Santeria* community, and he told me that he thought I might be having spontaneous contacts with the *Orishas*.

I think that I have made plain that at this point I didn't know what Santeria was, and for all I knew, an *Orisha* was a kind of fish.

He pointed out several books to me–especially the invaluable book *Santeria* by Migene Gonzalez-Wippler–made a few suggestions about how to behave toward the situation, and I left with my purchases.

After doing some reading, I constructed a crude altar–crude because I still hardly knew what colors or images to use–and began efforts to talk to "it."

I will refer to this phenomenon/concept/spirit simply

as "it" both because of the ambiguities involved in any kind of spirit manifestation, and because I was still groping in the dark. And the only method of communication that "it" would respond to was the pendulum I had used originally.

Through the same sort of painstaking questioning described earlier, "it" communicated that it wanted a very specific altar arrangement and some tools that I did not possess. I was told that it required the figure of a head (see the section on Eleggua) and a set of divinatory tools called *obi* (instructions for this also later). The statue was not so problematical as the *obi*, since traditionally these were four lobes of cola nut. I don't know what *your* supermarket carries, but to this day I have been unable to find this item in Los Angeles. Sometimes four pieces of fresh coconut are used as a substitute, but keeping a divination tool in the refrigerator didn't appeal to me.

Not only did "it" tell me what to get, but where to get it. There were several large import stores in various parts of the area in which I lived, but to visit all of them would take all day, so I asked "it" in which specific place I could find what I needed. Not only was it correct, but on visiting the other stores over the course of the next week or so I saw that indeed the one I was directed to was the only one that carried what I needed. This sort of thing was to become commonplace.

I obtained a carved African head, with an extremely high forehead, rather like a UFOnaut from Kenya. Not only was this symbolically appropriate in my mind, but it was the only such bust that they had. I looked for shells as a substitute for the cola nut, since this is also a traditional divinatory tool, but found none. What I did find–and still use–were beads of flattened black glass of the sort put in aquariums or in arrangements of dried flowers.

In the seances with "it" that followed, I was instructed how to anoint the figure with perfumes (a practice I later discovered was common in Greek paganism) and how to use the *obi*. Two things are interesting here. The "spirit" flatly refused to communicate through tarot cards or the *I Ching*, both of which I had used almost twenty years. I asked myself that if I was communicating with a part of my unconscious as some occultists theorize (or dogmatically state) why did "it" not use these? Why speak to me through an African system I had no knowledge of. "It" refused to have anything to do with this material for almost six months–as though it needed to *learn*. Secondly, I was to discover that the magicians of traditional people frequently walked off into the wilderness and returned with rituals, the power to heal, foretell the future, etc., with no access to books or teachers, but being instructed *directly by the spirits*.

Experiences like those described above, combined with recurring dreams, became so intense that I returned to the occult store to get a referral to a *Santeria* center where I could receive initiation. I felt so emotionally compelled by the experience that I was willing to present myself, your basic W.A.S.P., to a group of strangers in an alien ethnic subculture and ask to join the club, if–and I am not being facetious–we could even speak the same language. He told me that a *Santeria* (*Santeria* priestess) was a regular customer and he would ask her advice. He was kind enough to follow through his promise, and he took the trouble to call me at work with her response.

Her reply, roughly paraphrased, was: "Tell the white boy not to do it." I was rather surprised, not to say disappointed, but in years to come I was to find a few good reasons for her response. Despite the way it sounds these reasons were, for the most part, not based on race. She fully encouraged me to practice the magic on my own, but the *Santeria* community itself, even assuming I could have penetrated it at that state of my knowledge, was highly political and not altogether benign. They both felt I was too naive to get involved–and in time I came to agree.

In the meantime, in mundane life, I became part of a mass firing from an organization that, at the time, did not seem long for this world. I was far from happy, but not immediately worried because my savings, severance pay, and unemployment award were quite healthy. But not only were these the Reagan Prosperity years–when so many people fell out of the middle-class–but we were in the middle of the longest writer's guild strike in Hollywood history, so my other industry contacts were useless. They were laid off too!

*Chapter 4*

# TELL MY HORSE—
# GO BACK TO MISSOURI

As you may remember from those wonderful years (around 1985), things got worse quickly. I must have interviewed at every talent agency still open (damn few) and several studios. The market, thanks to Reagan and the strike, was tighter than a new bride and my savings were slowly becoming cosmic ash. I continued my magical experiments, but I was "told" repeatedly that things were not getting better soon. In fact, I was warned of my firing through a dream the week it happened.

What happened was this: I had been assiduously avoiding making any "psychic predictions" regarding my personal situation. This was partly due to normal human cowardice, but mostly from a feeling of helplessness that, when the office situation deteriorated, there might not be any place to go. Readings that I had done for other people on similar topics had been depressingly accurate.

I went to bed one night after another dismal day watching the company hold on by its fingernails. I was presented with a dream in which I stood by a grave and watched a black coffin being lowered into the earth. When I woke up there was no question in my mind that this was my last week of work. I still hadn't been given any kind of notice, or even a hint, but then, neither had anybody else who had been axed. Sure enough, on Friday evening I was informed that that was it.

Months went by and I came to the genuinely horrifying conclusion that I was going to have to go home for a while until the strike ended or something else happened to change things. I'm sure you know what I mean by "home"–that place we all leave in varying degrees of ecstatic relief. In my case, it meant a return to the Midwest after ten years in southern California.

In the middle of winder.

It was no consolation to me that a multitude of others were in the same boat. You may have seen some of the inhuman interest stories on *60 Minutes* and its sibling shows: grotesque interviews with mothers saying to the camera, "If he's living under my roof, he follows my rules. That means no girls in his room and no staying out after ten. I don't care if he *is* thirty-five." This usually with the humiliated son standing in the background.

As I was packing my possessions, I received a sort of benediction from the "spirit." It was only a few days from my departure. Most of my possessions had already been boxed for shipping and my airline reservations had been made. I still had my little "Voodoo altar" set up on a cloth on the floor printed with a Catholic religious scene. I was in the kitchen doing some final cleaning when I heard an impact and a light tinkling sound coming from the living room. I went to check on the noise, and saw a hole the size of a grade AAA grapefruit in one of the panels of my floor to ceiling windows. I thought that someone had thrown a rock and I turned to look for it.

Earlier I had done a tarot card reading for myself, in which, appropriately, the Devil and the Wheel of Fortune were prominent (those adept at tarot will find some little humor in this) and it was laid out in front of the African bust and other magical fetishes that I used. There was no rock, or baseball, or even a grapefruit.

What there was–its neck broken and its head laying square on the Devil trump–was a pure white dove. This is the part of the story some people simply don't believe–even people intimately familiar with "psychic phenomena." It sounds just a bit too much like a bad movie. Nevertheless, it is true. Those of you familiar with the traditions of both magic and paganism are aware of the significance of a white dove as a holy offering. Those of you familiar with urban areas know the odds against a white dove–as opposed to a pigeon–thinking my third story window was a piece of sky.

I tore its head off and drenched the bust and my instruments in its blood.

This is the place where people not raised in the tradition have problems: the blood offering. For now I will confine myself to the narrative, but since animal offerings are an integral part of Voodoo traditions, it will be discussed in greater detail later.

So home I went–luckily for a much shorter time than expected. About this four-month period there are two events related to our subject.

I have at times been asked, regarding the practice of any kind of magic, "what good does it do you really?" Hopefully this book will go a long way to answer that in concrete terms (as opposed to mystical nonsense). It has been my habit, for years my habit, for years before the "Voodoo" experiences began, to read the tarot cards every morning. I did this both for prognostication an as a mental exercise. As I said earlier, there was a six month period when "*ifa*" would not respond through this system. This period had passed just before my move, and I was in the habit of speaking to the "spirit" through this technique as well as the pendulum.

The day before this occurrence I had made an appointment for a job interview. My plan was to stay in the Midwest just long enough to make some money, wait for the situation to change in California, and then return to civilization. In any case, I had this interview set up and went to bed early to make sure that I was fresh for it. I then had a rather intense nightmare in which I was in a serious automobile accident. This could have symbolized any number of things, so I wasn't alarmed.

After showering, I performed my usual morning ritual and asked (through the pendulum) if the spirit would predict the events of the day for me. It said that it would. I then asked if it would speak through the tarot. It refused. After questioning, the only oracle that it would speak through was the Chinese *I Ching,* an unusual choice, I thought, for an African spirit.

So I threw the *I Ching,* holding in my mind particularly the question of my afternoon interview. The answer I received was: hexagram twelve, "obstruction" changing to hexagram six, "contention." This did not bode well for the interview.

As you may have guessed, I had the traffic accident predicted in the dream and by the oracle. On top of that, my license was being renewed, so I spent several hours in jail while they tried to decide whether I was driving without a license or not (hence the hexagram "contention"). The irony in this, as in all such stories, is that If I had heeded the warning and stayed home that day, I would have had no proof that the prediction was genuine.

This disaster, too, passed, and I began to want out of the situation even more desperately than I thought I would. I began an operation to obtain a job that would allow me to make enough money to return to the coast. During these conjurations my distaste for the Midwest was uppermost in my mind.

The following week I received a letter from an agent I knew informing me of an opening at a management company in West Hollywood. I knew the man who owned the office, called, got the job, and was back in Los Angeles within three weeks.

*The Hollywood sign*

*Chapter 5*

# DEAD MEN WORK IN THE FIELDS OF HOLLYWOOD

I became established back in the Hollywood area and worked in an office in the fashionable Sunset Plaza district just outside of Beverly Hills. Once again I was able to spend my work time around actors and writers whose company I dearly loved. Unfortunately the man who owned the management company was a failed actor who turned his spectacularly mediocre talent to screaming at casting directors over the phone and finding scapegoats for the fact that he had no idea what he was doing. Don't get me wrong–he and I got along just fine. But having to breathe the effluvia of his daily rages was a little wearing. I will return to this point shortly.

Having settled, I resumed my magical experiments and the study of Afro-Caribbean magic. I had taken a bit of a break while I was away–try to find a well-stocked metaphysical bookstore in Kansas City.

I learned long ago that one of the most useful tools in any occult practice, whether dealing with "spirits" or direct work on the self, is the ability to go into trance. The simplest means of becoming adept at this is to learn the techniques of hypnosis. Surprisingly, only a few practitioners of my acquaintance have every bothered with this, partly because they are unwilling to work to become adept at it–and it does require work–but also because of an almost Victorian superstitious fear.

The technique that I used, and still use, involves a lengthy trance induction–not using a tape by the way, the method is active not passive–followed by the attempt to communicate with the spirit or force I want. This has sometimes produced ecstatic psycho-physical states, spontaneous healings or "poltergeist" effects. Using this technique, at least four times a week, I attempted to improve communication with the spirit guide that I still vaguely thought of as "ifa." Now *Ifa* is not, I discovered, considered one of the *Orishas*. That is, not normally a spirit that communicates with mankind directly (according to *Santeria* theology) and I had always though that the identification of what I was talking to was a bit muddled. So my main goal was greater sensitivity as a medium, and cleaner, more direct communication.

One work day, after an evening spent in this kind of exercise, lunch hour came and I decided to spend part of it at one of the classier bookstores in town. I went in and began browsing. In the fiction section, I had the strange experience of becoming "stuck." I had idly picked up a copy of William Gibson's *Count Zero*, thumbed through it and put it back. I had never read any of Mr. Gibson's work—which I had associated with boring speculation about computers—and wasn't interested that day. I turned to leave the store, and couldn't. I literally couldn't bring myself to take that step out the door. I kept wandering around, watching my lunch hour trickle away. My back hurt, and I had to pee, but I still couldn't leave. Finally, with five minutes left in my lunch break, I went back, picked up *Count Zero*, bought it and left. I felt a physical pressure ease.

Later, when I began to read the book, I had one of those eerie sensations of being manipulated or tricked that are so common when dealing with spiritist phenomena. *Count Zero*—which takes place in the next century—was indeed about computer technology, being one of the pioneer novels in the "cyberpunk" wave of science fiction. What I did not know when I bought the book, was that as part of the plot, the daemons of Haitian Voodoo manifested themselves in the worldwide computer net, called "cyberspace"—a technological equivalent of the astral plane of occult theory.

Early in the story there occurs a pun on my name in relationship to the Voodoo spirit *Legba*. It was so direct that if the author had been an acquaintance, I would have assumed it to have been a deliberate joke. I looked up Legba in my references and found that he was associated with exactly the sort of phenomena and talents that the spirit had manifested. During the next seance

I asked if it was identifying itself as Legba. The answer was "yes." I asked for another "sign" to assure me my conclusions were correct. I had some errands to run, so I left home, and, while walking down the street, my eye was caught by something on the sidewalk. It was a dollar bill held down by a colorful bird feather and cowry shell that have been cut and filed to be part of a set of *caracoles*–the traditional divination system of *Santeria*. This was in an area swarming with street people, and yet it remained untouched until I picked it up. The shell, feather, and money together had the look of an *Ebbo*, an offering or spell to the spirits of Voodoo. I supposed I had my answer.

That was neither the first time nor the last that an important question was answered by strange synchronicities involving a book I had never read. Both Robert Anton Wilson and Colin Wilson have written about similar experiences in the course of their work.

Back at the office, my employer continued to scream into the telephone to camouflage his general lack of business acumen. Being around this eight hours a day was making me a nervous wreck. After a particular bad day, I decided to see what could be done about it.

While he was out, I picked up one of his absent-mindedly scrawled notes and took it with me as a "magical link", that is, a personal object that theoretically maintains an Etheric link with the person who owned it.

At home I took the note to my altar and began the trance-induction and invocation ritual that had come to be my basic procedure. I placed the "link" underneath a drawing of the veve or graphic symbol of Legba and proceeded to make my request. I spoke out loud and (I think this is important) and explained the situation as though I were talking to another person in the room. In the tradition of Voodoo magic, especially the Haitian variety, there are techniques whereby another man's spirit can be "bound" with the help of familiar spirits, especially if he is considered to have behaved aggressively toward the magician. Basically, I requested that the man I worked for be constrained from making his crazy outbursts and behave like a civilized adult. I then placed the link underneath the talisman consecrated to Legba, and placed both in a small wooden box. I closed the ritual and went to sleep.

When he walked in the following morning, he had a glazed look in his eyes and he moved rather slowly, as though drugged. He complained of a lack of energy and fuzzy-headedness. He left early that day, thinking that he might be coming down with something.

He wasn't. From that day until I left for a better position three or four months later his behavior was completely changed. His outbursts almost completely disappeared. When I left I destroyed the magical link, and was later told that his old behavior patterns had returned.

Immediately after the successful manifestation of the spell, I began to feel rather tired myself. This was not a flu, but a general lowering of energy that I couldn't shake. It finally dawned on me that I had neglected to do what any Santero or Haitian Bocor would have done to start with: feed the spirit that was doing me the favor. According to tradition, aside from the appropriate animal offerings that I did not have access to (it's hard to get a live chicken in the city) Legba was supposed to be appeased by the spine and tail bones of food animals. This was because, as lord of the roadways and information, the spinal cord which carries so many nerve impulses to and from the brain was within his natural province.

I went to the local market that catered to the Hispanic community, and which had a butcher who could provide out-of-the-ordinary cuts of meat. I bought a section of spinal cord which I placed on the altar. I asked if this was acceptable, and the answer was "yes." I asked (through the pendulum) how long it should remain. It said, "nine days." This did not thrill me, but I put the offering in a sealed container and followed instructions. The malaise from which I had suffered lifted instantly.

Psychosomatic? I can't argue the point. I know only that the phenomenon was not something I expected. The energy to cause the "magical" change I desired had to come from somewhere. Since I had not fed the spirit, he was obliged to take it from me.

All of this, I have to insist, was not coincidence, as it involved a personality change in my employer with no apparent cause and totally at variance with what had been for years his normal behavior. This followed, point for point, the requests I had made the evening before.

The more material I accumulated on the various Voodoo traditions–Haitian, *Santeria* and *Macumba*–the wider my experimentation went. I learned some of the traditional methods of Afro-Caribbean divination and tried to see if there was anything else floating around in the aether that would talk to me.

By this time I had departed to a large extent from the "psychological" view of spirit phenomena made popular in the last twenty years of so–the notion that it was all "the collective unconscious" or some such thing. I had come to the conclusion that the entire "Voodoo" experience began with me in the first place because–completely unbeknownst to me–I was living in an area where such things were practiced and those specific spirits–or things that answered to those names, were called up. In short, I lived in their neighborhood, and being an experienced medium, one of them came by to make my acquaintance. Maybe this sounds too literal to you. I will defend my position later.

I had identified what I considered a class or "family" of intelligences referred to in the Haitian tradition as Lords of the Crossroads–like Legba–and in *Macumba* as Eshus and in *Santeria* as Elegguas. All, it seemed to me, were different names for the same class of beings. I selected a spirit called Eshu Marabo, one that could perform healings, bring luck, defend the magician, and so forth. This was partly to further my career, but partly just to see what would happen. It became a rather cute, but frustrating, relationship with what religious historians refer to as "the trickster." The family of Eshus (sometimes spelled Exu) were generally considered devils, which made the whole thing even more attractive to me.

The *Orishas* of *Santeria* and *Macumba* are basically the same. They come from the *Yoruba* tradition while the Haitian spirits go by what are largely Dahomean names. From the Brazilian literature there is a whole constellation of graphic talismans and signs used in the magic. Most of his cannot be obtained in the U.S. and I will supply some of that obscure material in this book. One of the reasons I selected Eshu Marabo was that he was one of the few Eshus for whom I could find a magical signature.

I began with pendulum divination to decide what would be an appropriate way to propitiate the spirit. Somewhat to my horror, the oracle insisted on the heavy use of cigars rather than incense as a fumigant. As a lifelong non-smoker, I had visions of making myself sick at each conjuration, but this is what it said, so I went along.

None of the Voodoo traditions are purely African. The Carib Indians used tobacco in their rituals and this was picked up by the black slaves imported by the colonists. This, along with offerings of rum and perfume (which I was also instructed to use) have been an integral part of the magic ever since.

I performed the conjurations at least five times a week, requesting money, status, and a number of personal things. I must say that I was not impressed by the response to my specific requests, but there was enough genuine strangeness to make me believe that I had conjured something–Marabo or not.

I began seeing apparitions. These usually occurred at random times during the daylight hours. On one particular occasion, I was on my way to work, heading down the stairs of my apartment building, when, turning the corner at the stairway landing, I saw a *figure* of a man leaning over the railing above looking at me. I say the figure of a man, because that's all there was. He was transparent and a sort of tan or smoky color, like the hologram of a mannequin. I stopped, we "looked" at each other, and he faded away. The hallway was well lit with both light fixtures and the mid-morning summer light coming through a large nearby window. There were no shadows from people walking by–no one else was in the hallway. I looked at it for a long time–close to half a minute–before it disappeared. It was as if it wanted to be sure it had been seen.

While this was happening, a friend of mine, an experienced technician in the video industry, was being harassed by his employer. The strategy was apparently to force old personnel to resign so the company could avoid paying the benefits. He was also involved with an occult group that I frequented and wanted to try an experiment to protect his situation. I told him to bring a "link" with the person or persons harassing him. I performed a ritual to ask what, exactly, to do for my friend. I was told that he should being a potted plant as a focus for the "spell."

We met at the home of a mutual friend and performed a ritual of protection cobbled together from what I knew. He took the "link" and buried it in the potted earth. The spirit said that so long as he took care of the plant, his job would be intact and his persecutors would get retribution. According to his testimony, it worked.

I continued to make requests regarding my personal glorification and enrichment. These were answered in average terms. Strange things would happen but they seemed like efforts by an inferior spirit trying to appease me and look big–something of which may of the old magical texts warn.

For example, I requested money. As it happened, I also needed a new wallet. Walking in front of my office building I saw, laying on top of a newspaper vending machine, a brand new wallet, apparently never used. It was the same style and size of my old one, even to the color. Coincidence. Fine. But I had never seen a new wallet sitting in the open ignored by passersby as though it was invisible.

That same day, after work, I walked down the hill to the aforementioned Bodhi Tree bookstore. On the way, something caught my eye underneath the leg of a bus bench. I bent down to pick it up, and it was a ten dollar bill. I continued to the used book section of the Bodhi Tree and found a copy of a book that I had not seen in nearly twelve years, and never in that store. It was *Macumba, Teachings of Maria-Jose, Mother of the Gods*, by Serge Bramly. It cost ten dollars.

The frontispiece to chapter one was a graphic representation of one of the spirits. It was Eshu Marabo.

In addition to this, during one ritual, a stone weighing just under two pounds crawled slowly nearly a foot across a level altar table.

The final straw on all this utterly useless psychic silliness came when, frustrated at the lack of positive results, I asked what I could do to increase the spirit's power in the physical world. The response was that I should pile the altar with yams and smoke more cigars.

This was really too much. I dismissed the spirit and burned the related talismans, thanking it for the wallet and the book, and pointing out that it had done nothing that I requested.

It should be noted that yams are a traditional offering–along with animals–in both Afro-Caribbean magic, and in the original African religions. It should also be noted that during the period of this experiment–two months or more–I began to smoke more and more cigars during the ritual. I was and am not a smoker. I got the distinct feeling that the spirit–whatever it was–was using me to enjoy sensations that it couldn't, and tried to keep me satisfied with little tricks. This sort of thing is not unknown in either the occult literature or psychic research.

Do I think it was really "Eshu Marabo"? Probably not. People shouldn't put too much faith in conjurations or symbols on their own. I saw enough to think "something" was there. What it was I have no idea. Whatever it may have been, it was nothing I needed.

Eventually I went on to a "better position" than working in a personal management firm. I have to say that the improved position was due to an answered request from whatever it was that wanted to be called Legba. I performed the ritual as described and made a detailed request regarding money, location and atmosphere. I repeated this for several nights. Within the month I was informed by a director I knew of just the kind of opening I had requested. I interviewed after work and was immediately accepted for the job. The next day I was preparing to give notice, when the owner informed me that due to financial problems he was closing the office in a week.

I had been saved from trouble that I didn't even know was coming. This sense of "protection" or "good luck" has increased as time has gone by.

*Chapter 6*

# SPIRITS THAT FINDETH HIDDEN TREASURE

Up to now I have concentrated on "phenomena" and practical results rather than metaphysical theory. So few books on magic contain such accounts, because, I am afraid, many authors are non-practitioners. I know of sever such–writing on anything from Crowley to the Golden Dawn to Wicca–who have never practiced magic in their lives. They usually justify this by confusing magic with religion, and by telling the reader that it's all a form of Jungian psychology, or quantum physics. This is called "psychologizing" or "scientizing" and are usually attempts by frightened people to make unfamiliar things familiar.

In my opinion this is fraudulent, although usually not consciously so. The truth is, the average Science of Mind practitioner practices more real magic than many self-proclaimed "initiates" or "adepts." This is not to say that there aren't individuals and groups that use these techniques to lead successful lives. There are; I have met them. But the cultural phenomenon of the "adept' who can't pay the rent and whose phone has been shut off for non-payment, is common enough that I had to point it out before proceeding. This book exists largely as an antidote to that attitude.

I had come to a time when I needed a sum of money rather badly. I had been laid off due to the slack season in the television industry and was living a bit tighter than I liked. Whatever my work options, I needed the money sooner rather than later. I did not need a tremendous sum: two thousand dollars would solve my problems nicely.

While I had manipulated job circumstances and created general runs of luck, I had never made a serious effort to produce raw cash–one of the prime suspects of the old Grimoires. Since I had a lot of time on my hands, I had nothing to lose in making this time-honored attempt.

I set up a more elaborate altar than usual (instructions for this later). While finding the appropriate candles I discovered that, due to the large Hispanic population, genuine *Santeria* candles could be found in the most surprising places–even supermarkets. Of course, most of the people who bought them thought that they were Catholic votive candles–although how they explained the one labeled "seven African powers" I have no idea.

After I had constructed the altar with what I considered to be the correct symbols and tools, I began each session with a full cleansing–or banishing ritual–based on the type described in the Golden Dawn, and censed the area of operation. I anointed the African head that was the "home" of the spirit with perfumed oil, and then induced an auto-hypnotic trance using a large piece of rock crystal as a visual focus.

Then I called up the spirit, and said exactly what I needed and why. Through the pendulum, the African *obi*, and the tarot, I would hold a "conversation" with the spirit. Answers to questions would pop into my head at unexpected moments.

I was "told" during a several day repetition of this lengthy exercise, that my layoff would continue for longer than expected (this turned out to be correct). Therefore, it said, I would have to make a direct appeal for the money as a gift. From whom, I would like to have known. Using the pendulum, I went through every option that I could think of. Finally, at a loss, the image of an aunt appeared in my mind. I asked if this was the person to approach. The response was "yes." I could hardly believe this because the woman was notoriously tight-fisted, and I would not have dreamed of requesting fifty dollars much less two thousand.

She, the oracle insisted, was the one.

In addition, the spirit insisted that the spell would not be successful unless a proper offering of "food" were made. It wanted the offering of a live animal, and would accept no other. After my experience with the cattle spine, I took this suggestion seriously. Since my options were rather limited, I obtained a "feeder rat" from a large pet supply store. These rodents are bred as food for large reptiles such as boas, and are available at low cost in many pet stores.

At this point, I am going to describe something that, at first, I had not intended to write about, but after some discussion with a friend, I decided that honesty was the most important thing, so here it is. In the tradition of Afro-Caribbean magic, especially of the darker variety, there are a number of spells involving the immolation of sacrificial animals in rather grisly ways. After many hours of seances with the pendulum and other devices, I was quite specifically told that the animal *must* be disposed of in a very specific way if the spell was to work. This required dropping the animal alive in a pot of boiling water. It sounds far worse than it was, and the animal died instantly, but I was in a sweat by the time it was over.

I cut its head off quickly with a very sharp knife, and spread the blood on the graphic image of Legba and the statue. Then I placed a tiny smear of blood on a postal envelope.

I carefully drafted a letter to my aunt. I consecrated the letter as a talisman by calling up Legba, asking his blessing, and, while holding the woman's image in my mind, telling him to travel with the letter to her home and touch he mind in my favor. I placed the letter in the blooded envelope, and mailed it.

The oracle continued to insist, in response to my repeated neurotic inquiry, that all would be well. As an additional test, I asked the pendulum when the money would arrive. It said exactly nine days. I noted the information and waited.

I received a phone call shortly thereafter from the aunt. To my complete shock, she had no objection to giving me the money. She was even willing to transfer it directly into my bank account. *And the money arrived in my hands in nine days–not just to the day, but literally to the hour–as predicted.*

On the grimmer side, the building I was living in had changed its "policy," which allowed a large number of people to become residents under what is known as "Section 8"–that is, on welfare. I have nothing but sympathy for people in this situation, but unfortunately, I was soon surrounded by violent types–the people who had moved next door were crack dealers.

I am libertarian enough not to object to such things on moral grounds. To do so would be complete hypocrisy considering my own experimentation with such things in the past. What I objected to was the violence. Every day I heard altercations, threats of murder, beatings, and the distinct sound of revolver being loaded. I was awakened out of a deep sleep by the sound of a person being violently knocked to the floor.

I spoke to the manager of the building, and she said she was in contact with the police. Nothing happened. I talked to the narcotics division of the police department. Nothing happened.

Then I had another of those warnings like the kind I received before the traffic accident.

One night I had a dream of a black woman crouching inside my open apartment door.

I woke up screaming.

Since I do not suffer from inordinate fear of black women, it seemed to have been the open door that disturbed me. I got up, went to work (the layoff was over) and tried to forget about it.

I was proceeding with my magic and clairvoyant experiments, and the next time I performed my trance/ritual exercise, instead of the usual ecstatic feelings I had feeling of foreboding. I asked the pendulum if I was being warned of something. "Yes," it said. I threw the *I Ching*.

A *festival altar*

Its response was: hexagram twenty-three, "splitting apart." Perhaps more significantly, in another translation it is called "stripping away." Those of you who have read Robert Anton Wilson's *Cosmic Trigger* (New Falcon Publications, 1993) or his *Illuminatus Trilogy* will be amused by this. As John Dillinger said, it was one of *those* coincidences.

The next day was a day off. I did my usual morning tarot reading and had the worst reading I have ever had, before or since. I have lost the note with the exact order of the cards, but I remember which cards came up.

Ten of Swords, Nine of Swords, Three of Swords, Five of Swords, Ten of Wands, The Tower, Five of Coins, Five of Cups, all rounded out with some court cards. Those of you familiar with tarot will realize that nearly the only negative cards left out of the reading were Death

and the Devil and from my point of view these are not necessarily negative.

I had been warned four times in various ways that something bad was coming, supposedly on that very day. How did I deal with this? Of course! I talked myself out of it. This is our Judeo-Christian psychology at work. If you have clairvoyant talent, by the time you learn to use it, you've already been psychologically castrated. Anyone raised in a culture with psychic traditions intact would have known how to deal with the information. This, of course, is what European anthropologists and missionaries refer to as "superstition" and "magical thinking."

I had some shopping to do, and wanted to take in a movie. As I was preparing to leave a man came to my door and informed me that he needed to do a little work on my ceiling. This seemed perfectly legitimate, as such work had been ongoing in the building for some time.

I left, telling him to lock the door when he left the apartment.

When I returned that evening, I found the knob–but not the dead bolt–locked. As I entered, I saw that I had been robbed.

Some electronics and some leather coats had been taken. Oddly, some art supplies were also stolen, but not the valuable stuff. What was enraging was the fact that the door had not been forced. After several days I concluded that the greasy little bastard that worked on my ceiling stayed until lunch hour, and not wanting to bother his supervisor, and not giving a damn, saved himself the trouble by leaving my door unlocked.

I also discovered–through loose lips of the culprits–that it was the crack dealers next door who had done the job. They simply listened for the workman to leave for lunch, tested the door, went in and were out in five minutes. When questioned by the police, the workman's supervisor denied that any workman had even been on my floor that day.

I will save any comment about the incompetence of the Los Angeles Police Department (LAPD) for another place. Suffice it to say that reports were lost, and fingerprints were ignored.

So, while the police were busy gearing up for the Rodney King incident to come nearly a year later, I had to deal with the situation myself. I had, as I said, discovered who had done it. It didn't take Sherlock Holmes when all you had to do was listen to the ramblings of people fucked up on good crack and bad wine at 3 a.m., probably having been awake for four days straight.

I decided to try an old technique common to all forms of witchcraft. I went to the old Hollywood Memorial Park on Santa Monica Boulevard, and got a jar full of grave mold. As payment to the lords of the cemetery, I left a bottle of good rum high in the branches of a tree near the grave–it may be there still.

I took the material to my altar and prepared two talismans of a rather nasty nature. These were taken from *The Sacred Magic of Abramelin the Mage*, a Grimoire made popular by MacGregor Mathers and Aleister Crowley.

First I performed a ceremony to "charge" the material basis of the spell. Then I placed the two Abramelin talismans under the carpet in the hallway and, each day as I left for work, I scattered the grave mold before the doors of the people I wanted gone.

In addition I performed an evocation of one of the "lords of the cemetery," Baron Samedi or Baron Cimetere, or Baron LeCroix, whatever name you call him (or them, they may be brothers), registered my complaint to "him" and sent him into the next apartment to deal with the people who had wronged me.

Two weeks later, the man's wife left with their baby. This deprived him of his welfare benefits and thus, his rent. About two weeks later, my other target, the people across the hall who spent most of their time screaming, moved out. Not long after, the police finally decided to investigate the apartment next door–this was more than six months after the manager and I made our complaints–and all the parties went to prison. Oddly, I was not involved in this in any way. I was not called to testify, nor did the authorities even speak to me. This was in spite of the fact that I made at least one written complaint to the police.

It was as if the reports to the police had disappeared. I was free of both the unpleasant company of my neighbors and the worry of gang retribution.

*Divinatory tools*

*Chapter 7*
# DIVINATION TECHNIQUES

While divination is integral to all forms of magical practice, in the various Voodoo traditions it is more important than most, since any divination is an invocation of the gods.

In their original form many of the traditional African methods of divination are complex beyond belief. This is complicated by the fact that even in their new world forms much his still passed on verbally and therefore genuinely secret and not just obscure.

As this book is aimed at the self-taught practitioner who is not raised in a *Santeria* or *Macumba* community, I am limiting the methods to those that are both effective and relatively simple.

There are five basic methods of divination used in the Afro-Caribbean traditions:

1. THE TAROT CARDS
2. THE PENDULUM
3. THE OBI
4. THE CARACOLES (Cowry Shells).
5. POSSESSION (Altered States of Consciousness).

## TAROT CARDS

These are used primarily by the magicians of Haiti, although cards are used in *Macumba* and *Santeria* as well. There is also a pack called "the Spanish playing cards" which evolved from the Tarot, but have the trumps and queens removed, leaving only forty-eight cards. I will not explain the Tarot here, as that would take an entire book. Those of you interested may purchase a standard deck (the Rider/Waite deck is most popular among beginners) and many books of instruction on serious divination with the cards and their magical connections refer to *The Way of the Secret Lover: Tantra, Tarot and the Holy Guardian Angel* by Christopher S. Hyatt, Ph.D. and Lon Milo DuQuette (New Falcon Publications, 1991).

## THE USE OF THE PENDULUM

The pendulum is a balanced weight suspended from a piece of string or a fine chain. A homemade pendulum can be made with rings or steel nuts. Particular care should be taken so that it is as balanced as possible. The author uses professionally made dowser's pendulums, usually made from machined brass or copper. They are either bullet or onion shaped, some with hollow spaced inside for what, in dowsing, is called "the witness." This is identical in concept to the magical link.

I have seen pendulums for sale in occult shops aimed at the "New Age" audience that were made from quartz crystal points attached to a chain. These are nearly useless as they are off balance and too light. I recommend that you take the trouble to find one that is professionally made. They are inexpensive, usually costing $20 or less in the United States.

The use of the pendulum is quite simple in theory, but you may find it takes some time and patience to "get it to work" for you. The temptation to "make" the pendulum tell you what you want to hear must be resisted.

For the purposes of spirit communication I have found the best method to be to have your arm (whichever you normally use to write with) solidly anchored, elbow on a table, or, if you are sitting on the floor in a cross-legged position, on your knee.

The classic method of the use of the pendulum–or rather to train your mind in the use of the pendulum–is to give it a little swing forward and back away from you in a straight line. You then ask the pendulum to give you a motion that indicated "yes" or "positive." The response is generally a clockwise circle, but this may vary. The process is repeated for "no" or "negative." In the event that this fails to work, an alternative is to tell the pendulum that a clockwise circle is "yes" and deliberately swing the tool in that direction, repeating the process with "no."

Most people who try this will get a response that becomes more sure and dependable with practice. A few will be instantly proficient. Others will feel unable to use the pendulum at all. If this happens, put the pendulum away until you feel some later "urge" to pick it up again. I have found that once the suggestion is planted, some people who demonstrated no ability, will, after some time suddenly find themselves proficient–with no intervening practice.

*Wooden Divinatory Board for Radiesthesia*

The test of any divinity system is the accuracy of the information it provides. Until you have confidence in this or any other method the answers should always be tested and not just assumed to be correct.

Another classic method of using the pendulum is with a kind of Ouija board set up, with the letters of the alphabet and numbers written in either an arc or a circle with lines drawn from these to the center of the board. The pendulum is held over this and questions are asked to which words are spelled out in response. This can be quite time-consuming and a strain on the arm. Occasionally boards like this can be found in stores readymade. Also books on a radiesthesia (the name for pendulum dowsing) sometimes contain charts of this kind that can be copied for use with a pendulum.

## THE OBI

The *Obi* consist of four flat objects that can be easily tossed. There must be a difference between each side–generally one is darker than the other. Traditionally the *Obi* have been four lobes of the cola nut, or four pieces of fresh coconut. A good substitute are the flat glass beads used for floral arrangements; these can be found in large import stores. White circles of paper can be glued to one side to form the color differentiation (paint tends to flake off glass). Alternately, coins can be used.

A question is asked that can be answered in some positive-negative fashion. This is actually more complex than "yes" or "no", and, if the *Obi* are thrown several times in succession a rather complex prediction can be achieved.

There are five possible patterns in which the *Obi* can fall in a single throw, each with a title and a meaning:

Generally the *Obi* are thrown once for any specific question, although a series of questions may be posed.

There are two exceptions to this: if *Alafia* (peace) or *Etawa* (struggle) comes up you must throw a second time to complete the answer. This only applies on a first throw. There are no more than two tosses. You may for example throw *Etawa* and for the second throw get *Alafia*. That (struggle becoming peace) is the answer. There are no further throws for that particular question.

The basic process is quite simple: Place yourself in a meditative and serious frame of mind, and cleanse the room in which you are working. In some Brazilian methods a fine chain or cord is placed in a circle around the area in which the *Obi* are to be thrown to define the sacred space. In Santeria the *Obi* are often cleansed in a bowl of exorcised water to make them pure. After asking the spirits, or a particular spirit to attend to your question, the *Obi* are tossed and the answer noted. The *Obi* can also be used in conjunction with the pendulum to gain more detail on the nature of the answer.

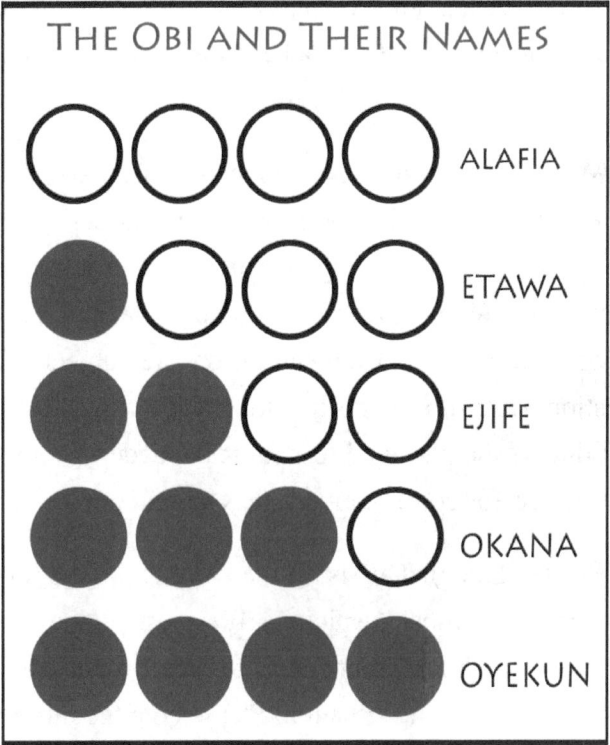

## THE MEANING OF THE ODU

The five patterns in which the *Obi* can land are called the *Odu*. The divinatory meanings of the *Odu* are:

ALAFIA (Peace). Broadly speaking, this is serenity and balance. The reader not familiar with the *Obi* will assume that this is the most auspicious *Odu* in the group because it consists of the most "positive" energy. In fact this is not quite the case since it is considered rather unbalanced. It is quiet and serene, yes, but if there is too much of it, it is also unfocused. Altogether a quiet, good omen, especially when it appears after a period of struggle. If *Alafia* appears on a first throw, the answer is incomplete and the *Obi* must be tossed again to complete the answer.

ETAWA (Struggle). As the name suggests, *Etawa* represents conflict. It could be conflict directly with a person or persons or struggle with a difficult situation. Confusion, things not in their proper place. This is a major or minor event depending on the subject of the question. Like *Alafia*, it is incomplete if it turns up on the first throw, and a second toss must be made to complete the answer, for conflict always has an outcome.

EJIFE (Balance). This is all the *Odu*, is the one that is considered the most auspicious. It represents the perfect balance of dark and light forces to create a harmonious, perfectly functioning situation. Please note the difference between this attitude and the Christian or Islamic one.

OKANA (Some good, some bad). This *Odu* one might consider the omen of the average day. It means that generally speaking all is (more or less) well. It implies that one element or incident may cause a less than satisfactory flow of events.

OYEKUM (Darkness). In the translation from the *Yoruba* this means "Full Twilight" but I have called it Darkness here as, to our minds, it reflects the meaning more clearly. It is the polar compliment to *Alafia*, being the negative power at its very height. In *Santeria* tradition, this *Odu* implies influences of the very worst kind. It is said that the divination should be abandoned at once, and a candle lit asking the protection of your ancestors. In its most benign sense, it can mean that the question cannot be answered.

## THE MEANINGS OF THE OMO ODU

If either *Alafia* (peace) or *Etawa* (struggle) are thrown first, a second throw must be made to complete the answer. Each of these combinations have separate meanings. These are called *Omo Odu*, meaning "children of the Odu."

I will begin with the *Omo Odu* resulting from a first throw of *Alafia*:

ALAFIA + ALAFIA This is the overwhelming presence of the "light" element, and the danger is laziness or drunkenness, or, on a milder note, complacency. If some task is to be accomplished, sobriety (in every sense) and concentration are urged.

ALAFIA + ETAWA This indicates a time of peace, contemplation, rest and planning before a test or struggle. It advises clear-headedness and emotional coolness if victory is desired in the coming difficult situation.

ALAFIA + EJIFE This is a good omen that combines cool-headedness and balance. It implies a "what will be, will be" attitude, and "what will be" is probably good.

**ALAFIA + OKANA**  This implies that no matter how much serenity and planning are represented by *Alafia*, *Okana* will throw a wrench into the works with one tiny unforeseen factor. Largely negative, implying great caution, or abandonment of the activity in question to another time.

**ALAFIA + OYEKUN**  The sudden unexpected occurrence of disaster, like going to the mailbox and being shot by a sniper. A warning of extreme caution, and also a warning that the dark elements cannot be calculated or accounted for.

**ETAWA + ALAFIA**  This implies a peaceful, satisfying situation that can only come about hard work and perhaps competition and struggle. You must earn your reward.

**ETAWA + ETAWA**  As the name of the *Odu* implies this is struggle after struggle. This is a situation of unrelenting effort before the desired goal is achieved. Any slacking means probable failure. In a lesser sense it can mean that nothing goes right no matter what you do.

**ETAWA + EJIFE**  This represents struggle or effort leading a perfect balance and a successful outcome.

**ETAWA + OKANA**  No matter how hard we work, our plans are fouled by one little event or element. This can mean frustration and failure after hard work, or in a more minor mode, working for perfection and getting mediocrity.

ETAWA + OYEKUN  The pressure of *Oyekun* makes this black as the ace of spades. We struggle and struggle only to meet with inevitable defeat. Our own energy is even used against us to our undoing. Find an honorable way to retreat–or just duck.

## THE TABLE OF IFA: THE CARACOLES

The use of cowry shells is the central technique of divination in *Santeria* and *Macumba*. The Haitian variety has a different national origin, and as a result of its history was isolated for nearly a century (they were denied diplomatic status by both the U.S. and Europe for a century because of white outrage at the idea of a successful slave revolt). The magic from Cuba, Puerto Rico, and the Virgin Islands spread to America (*Santeria*), and this like the tradition in Brazil (*Macumba*) had its roots in the Yoruba culture.

In the simplest version of its original form sixteen cowry shells were used as sacred divinatory tools. Several other objects were pulled blindly out of a bag to help determine the positive or negative slant on the reading.

All of this was usually done on a beautifully carved wooden tray with the face of *Ifa* himself staring out from the top (in Africa) or on a consecrated straw mat (in the U.S.). In Brazil a circle of chain or cord is used to define the sacred space.

One of the lords of the crossroads is called upon (see the chapter on Legba/Eshu) and the shells are thrown one or more times. The shells have been cut and filed so that they fall flat on one side or another like flipping a coin. There is another method using sixteen flat pieces of metal attached to a chain which is tossed rather like a horseshoe. To our knowledge this particular method is now used only in Africa, but it may still be practiced in some parts of Brazil.

In the case of the cowry shells, the serrated openings on the bottom are considered the mouths of the spirits, and only the shells facing up were counted to determine the answer.

Each number–from one to sixteen–of possible upward facing "mouths" had a "proverb" and a mythological story attached to it. There were also cleansing spells called *Ebbos* attached to each number. In addition, according to some authorities, there are as many as *five hundred* "secret" meanings attached to the system that to this day is passed on only orally.

For this reason I have created this simplified method that does not compromise the spirit of the system and is still possible for the beginner to learn. I emphasize that what I present here is a new adaptation of the "Table of Ifa" and not what one would be taught by an initiated *Santero* or *Macumba* priest.

*The Caracoles*

## HOW TO CONSTRUCT THE ORACLE

You will need sixteen cowry shells. (The traditional number is eighteen, but two are not used, being considered guardians of the oracle.) For the non-initiate practitioner, sixteen is all you need. These may be obtained from hobby stores, import stores, and on the internet.

The shells should be small, not the large kind often seen in coastal souvenir shops, about the size of a dime or a nickel. The humped backs of the shells must be ground down flat so that the shells have an even chance of landing on either side.

If you live in an area with African import stores, or real Botanicas, you may be able to find these shells easily, possibly with the hump already cut or ground down

You will also need a circular or square tray with a lip around the edge to prevent the shells from flying off when tossed. The tray must be square or circular and not oval or rectangular, as the flat area will be divided into four equal parts when the board is finished. The tray should be something more than a foot in diameter–eighteen inches to two feet is a good size. A medium sized pizza tray works well and can be purchased any place that sells kitchen utensils.

Paint the following design (or glue a copy of it) on the tray. (The colors, divisions and signs were determined through a seance using the pendulum, so this is a divination system produced through divination!)

## BOARD DESIGN FOR SHELL DIVINATION

In the upper left hand corner is the symbol of Legba, the lord of the crossroads, who opens doorways and conveys information. His symbol is painted white on a black background. This segment of the board represents positive, or benign male energy, and is particularly important in questions related to communication, travel, contracts and "white magic."

In the lower left hand corner is the symbol of Erzulie. It is painted black on an orange ground. This is positive female energy, and is important in questions regarding relationships, inspiration and all things related to the positive aspect of the astrological concept of Venus.

In the upper right hand corner is the symbol of Erzulie Dantor, also called Erzulie Ge-Rouge ("the red eyed"). This is painted black on a white ground. This

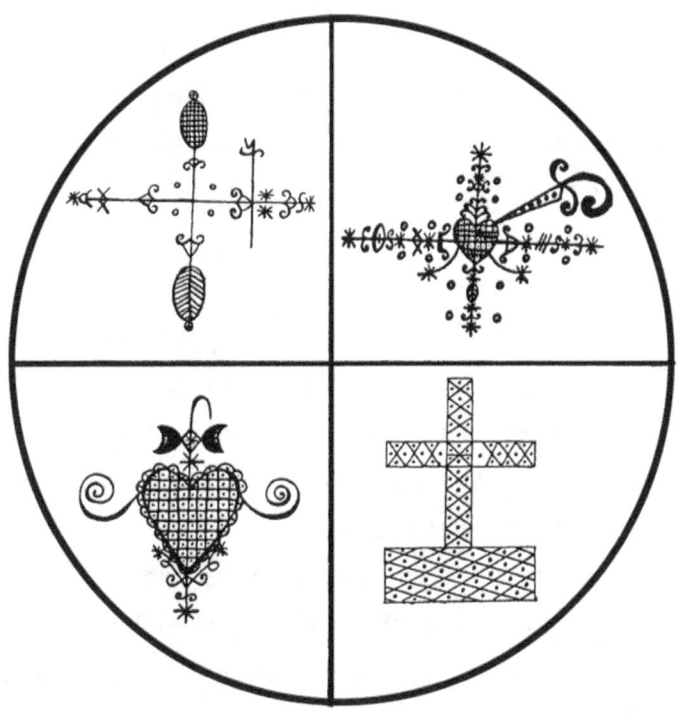

*Copy this Board Design, as instructed below.*

quarter of the board is important in matters of anger, hatred, jealousy and feelings of oppression. It is a negative female energy.

In the lower right hand corner is the symbol of Baron Samedi, which is painted black on red. This quarter represents negative or aggressive male energy. It is important in matters of "black magic," winning in competitions, defeating enemies, and all questions regarding death. Ironically Baron Samedi is also a healer, so this quarter of the board also speaks of regaining health from illness.

## THE MEANINGS OF THE ODU

In meanings given here are based upon the sixteen "proverbs." These meanings are also called *Odu* in the *Yoruban* language. These descriptions were developed for the system in this book and are based on the traditional meanings.

1. Mediocrity. Nothing much is happening or developing in this situation. Neither harm nor good.

2. Probable disagreement, competition, or conflict, possibly with a close associate or loved one. Contention and strife. Patience and serenity advised.

3. A conflict or argument leading to a deeply regrettable outcome. Implies the possibility of violence, accident or suicide as a result. Any conflict is to be avoided if possible. A good time to pursue solitary activity.

4. A mystery to be dealt with. The question cannot properly be answered as it is "covered over" by circumstances. Also implies unconscious motives and the world of dreams that cannot be handled with logic. Cultivate intuition and consult the spirits.

5. Having to do with the force of life itself, blood, health, fitness. In another sense the most basic and primitive motivations of a person or situation. A chance to deal with the fundamental forces of your life, physical or spiritual.

6. Seeking or standing up for the truth. A situation where no amount of subterfuge by you or another can

hide the truth of a statement or situation. Warns also to beware of lies by others.

7. The fundamental origin of any serious problem. It means you must deal with the hard to face basic facts of any recurring problem, either with yourself or others.

8. This says that the power of your thought is the most important factor in this matter. It can control and change circumstances and even your bodily health. The power of the mind over matter.

9. What you love best is killing you. This could be a bad love affair, a drug addiction or anything similar. It advises that this love must be given up. In another direction it can also mean that a close friend is betraying you behind your back.

10. The origin of a curse. The source of bad luck or "karma" must be dealt with. Guilt from the past must be eliminated. The source of bad energy and events must be eliminated from your life. You may also have been literally cursed and have to deal with that on its own level.

11. You are attempting to do something with inadequate tools or preparation. Whether within yourself or in the physical world you must have the right tools for the right job. Prepare more conscientiously and you will succeed.

12. There is conflict, even amounting to all out war. No relaxation is possible in this situation if victory is to be achieved. This could be in the outside world or within yourself.

13. Physical and/or spiritual purification is called for. Meditation, diet and environment are to be cleansed for improvement.

14. You are in a group or family where people envy you. Watch your words and your back.

15. Enthusiasm, religious experience, an overwhelmingly impressive and possibly joyous event. Whether positive or negative, the experience or emotion is potentially life changing.

16. Your intelligence and effectiveness will be multiplied if you seek other advice or sources of information. The answers are there, but you do not have all the information yet. Spread out your lines to bring in information. Network. Listen.

## HOW TO USE THE ORACLE

Wash your hands thoroughly before handling the shells, mentally imagining that this also cleanses your spirit.

Place the tray on an altar or on the floor. Greet the Master of the Crossroads and ask him to open a dialogue with the spirits so that they may answer you clearly and truthfully (see the section on Legba/Eshu).

If the divination is for another person present, they should be allowed to hold the shells and think about their question. The shells are then handed back to the diviner, held in both hands in a prayer-like position and tossed onto the tray.

First, count the number of shells that "speak." This

is the overall general answer to the question. It may be a direct answer, or take the form of advice, rather like the *I Ching*.

Now, examine and note each quarter division of the tray. Count the shells that speak in each separate answer. Any "speaking" shells that straddle the dividing black lines that quarter the tray are to be counted for the overall answer, but ignored for the reading of the four quarters.

The quarter of the board with the most speaking shells indicates the dominant force in the question. While the quarter with the fewest shells indicated the weakest force. The quarter with the most positive *Odu*, may show the way out of any implied difficulty.

Thus the shells can be read like a simplified astrological chart. For complex questions, this process can be gone through two or more times, but beware of trying to get the answer you want to hear. Any warnings given by the spirit can be quite serious.

As an example, if you receive a good *Odu* for the overall answer, but the majority of the "speaking" shells are in the upper right quarter ruled by Erzulie Dantor, it implies success, but with a great deal of emotional turmoil and contention in the process. The specific *Odu* contained in that quarter also adds more detail about the nature or cause of the turmoil.

With practice, this can form a detailed story in much the same way as the tarot and with the ability to give advice that typifies *I Ching* readings.

## POSSESSION AND ALTERED STATES OF CONSCIOUSNESS

The subject of possession is associated with terror and the demonic in Christian culture. (This apparently excludes "letting Jesus into your heart" which sounds suspiciously like demonic possession to me.)

Possession in the Voodoo traditions almost always occurs in group rituals, frequently after hours of preliminary ceremonies. While the average westerner assumes that possession is hypnosis or fraud, there are many documented cases of hostile witnesses who were spontaneously possessed while observing these rituals in Haiti, Brazil and other places. Almost without exception they suffered the amnesia, increased strength, and sometimes invulnerability to fire that typify the qualities of the spirit that claimed them. They would speak in the language of the place–whether they knew it or not–and serve the celebrants with advice, healing, and so forth as though a native. This usually caused great embarrassment and anger to the Christian skeptics to whom this occurred.

It may surprise the reader that religious possession, long considered psychosis by condescending observers, or demonic possession by meddling missionaries, is now considered normal by many ethnologists and appears in every culture where it is not suppressed or punished–as it is in ours.

Dr. Wade Davis, author of *The Serpent and The Rainbow* was honest enough to admit that he had witnessed phenomena involving possession that he could not explain, and courageous enough (considering his academic standing) to admit that the existence of spirits could not be disproved by science.

The film maker May Deren, in *Divine Horsemen*, an account of her study of Haiti, also tells how she experienced spontaneous possession by the spirit Erzulie on several occasions, acting as the goddess for the celebrants. Her amnesia after the experience was absolute. Ms. Deren seemed to suffer some embarrassment in writing about this, as she hid this remarkable experience in the back of the book in an appendix.

The symptoms of possession are roughly these: A numbing of the limbs, sometimes accompanied by involuntary movements or even convulsions. If this occurs the person undergoing the experience should only be touched enough to prevent him from injuring himself. Sometimes the experience may end at this point and no full possession takes place, otherwise another personality will manifest and a name should be demanded by the person presiding over the ritual. If cooperation is received, then the spirit can be consulted while in the body of the possessed person. If the spirit is unruly, or disoriented, or hostile, it should be banished firmly and with authority by the presiding magician. Traditionally bells are used for this as well as sprinklings with some consecrated liquid. This is an ancient practice in many cultures and one of hundreds copied by the Christian church.

*Meditation bells*

The formerly possessed person may feel physically exhausted afterwards, even for as much as a day. It is important that the spirit give verbal consent to leave the person, and not enter him again unless called by ritual.

For those who work alone, possession is highly unlikely and rather undesirable. However, if one is to attempt it, the western Judeo-Christian resistance to trance states in general–at least the kind involved in magic–must be overcome for the best results.

At its most successful, auto-hypnotic meditation techniques combined with magical ritual will enhance psychic functioning, and provide startling psycho-physical reactions that anthropologists refer to as "ecstatic." This is the sort of thing people of tradition experience when they travel to "the spirit world." Genuine out-of-body experiences occasionally but rarely occur.

To learn self-hypnosis requires patience and a commitment of time, but the technique itself is actually rather simple. It is possible to learn from a commercially produced tape, or by visiting a professional hypnotist.

I recommend that tapes be used as little as possible and the practitioner use his or her own voice. A full somnambulistic state is not the goal here, nor would it be useful when working alone.

## A SIMPLE SELF-HYPNOSIS TECHNIQUE

Sit in a straight-backed chair (do *not* lie down) in front of a table about the height of a desk. This can be done sitting cross-legged on the floor, but only if you can do this for up to an hour without discomfort.

Before this exercise, perform a cleansing ritual. The table should be set up a magical altar, and lit by candles even if in the daytime. The focus of the altar–whatever else may be on it–should be a crystalline object that reflects the light of the candles. I use a polished quartz crystal ball on a brass stand. As these can be expensive, quartz crystal points a little larger than your thumb are also useful. If you have a ball of lead-crystal glass, use that. The important thing is that it refract the light and quartz does that much better than clear glass.

Face the crystal with your eyes fixed on it and tell yourself in a whisper that you cannot take your eyes from it. Tell yourself that with each breath you take and each word you speak you are going deeper and deeper into trance. Tell yourself that your body is becoming rigid and unable to move, but utterly without tension of any kind.

Sound can be used as a background if you wish. Recordings of Tibetan monastic chants, for example, are available and are quite useful in this regard.

You will find your breathing changing at various times during this process. You should attempt to control and slow it only in the beginning. The deeper you go into trance the more you will find that your breathing changes in unexpected ways without interfering with your state. Let this happen. It may become swift, or shallow, or slow almost to imperceptibility. Similar descriptions can be found in the writings of Tantrik Yoga.

While staring at the crystal, tell yourself that your mind is lifting from your body into a higher, causal plane of being. Then tell yourself that you will count from one to ten, and, when you reach ten, all of your spiritual and psychic centers will open. Make this count slowly, one number to each breath.

Let the trance deepen. Do nothing for a while, and place no time limits on yourself unless absolutely necessary. For me, this time averages forty-five minutes to an hour.

When you feel your trance has deepened, tell yourself again that you will count from one to ten. In addition, suggest that in the crystal is the gateway to the spirit world and the being that you seek to communicate with (if that is indeed your goal). When you reach ten you will be even deeper in trance, and pass through the gateway to the spirit kingdom.

When this is done, relax into the hypnogogic experience of speaking with the spirit. Make no attempt to prejudge what you will see.

At any time during this process you may give yourself permission to move enough to use a pendulum, or read an appropriate invocation from a book. Do this slowly, so as not to spoil the state of trance. Return to the relaxed seated position when done.

When you consider that the ritual or meditation experience has run its course, bid farewell to the spirit and ask it to do work on your behalf. Then tell yourself that you will count backwards from five to one, and that when you reach one, you will be fully awake and relaxed carrying with you whatever power or spell you created in trance.

Ritually cleanse the space if you desire.

If you are patient and allot sufficient time to this practice—at least three times a week—the rewards will be great. The greatest barrier to get past is the tedium involved if the first few attempts don't meet your expectations. This *must* be ignored for a while. If you commit yourself to this practice for five days out of seven, by the end of the first week you will be pleased and surprised by the experience.

*Patience* and *commitment* are the keys to being very successful in this practice.

*Yoruba (Nigeria). Eshu/Elegba Image. Made of wood, cowry shells.*

*Chapter 8*

# THE LORDS OF THE CROSSROADS

I begin with the single most important class of beings in any of the Voodoo pantheons. These personalities are so numerous and so vital to the practice of the magic that I have given them a chapter all to their own.

The overall name for the spirit is Eshu, also called Eleggua, Elegba and (in Haiti) Legba, Kalfu and Baron Carrefour. These are the one and all of the class of spirits that must be called upon at the beginning of any ceremony, for any purpose, if one expects results. They are trickster spirits with a childlike sense of humor and a childlike cruelty (the exception is the Haitian manifestation of Legba, who appears as an old man. In Africa he remains a strong sexual figure).

The family of Eshus are solar-phallic in nature, frequently pictured with an erect phallus, or some object that symbolizes the same. They are masters of doorways, roadways, crossroads (where the physical and spiritual meet) and magic in general. They can be identified with the Greco-Roman Mercury (though not the dignified Thoth), and I have seen him convincingly compared to the Egyptian Set. He is often pictured as a young teenage boy, which should give you some idea of the sort of personality we are dealing with here.

His special day, according to *Santeria* and *Lucumi*, is Monday, although this kind of identification can vary (with all the spirits) depending not only on what country, but what part of what country you are in. The same variability applies to the saints that "mask" the spirits. For example, the saints used to disguise the spirits in New York are not always the same in Los Angeles or Brazil.

For Eshu the saint is often the Holy Child of Atocha, the Holy Guardian Angel, or St. Anthony. Colorful pictured candles are available for all of these. In Brazil the Eshus are identified with the Devil for reasons that will be explained. The colors of these spirits are black and red.

In Voodoo there are two different names for the spirits: Orisha (*Santeria/Lucumi*) and *Loa* (Haitian). They both refer to the emissaries of the creator god who were left on earth to interact with man. One of the several names of this creator is Olodumare and, according to myth, when he finished his work he became disgusted with physical existence and went elsewhere; thus, he is not to be invoked since one would receive no response. The detailed legends of each of these "gods" will not be gone into here except cursorily as this has been done exhaustively in several other volumes easily available. Also, the stories tend to vary wildly, although the personalities and powers of the spirits do not.

What is important in this regard about Eshu (and his many brothers and sisters) is that because of a particular favor he did for the creator, Olodumare said that he would grant him any favor, he had only to tell him what it was. Eshu never hesitated: "I want," he said, "to do whatever I will." Olodumare granted this. So to this day, of all the spirits, the Eshus are free of restriction. They are openers of doorways and communication with the gods, flingers of the darkest kind of curse and bringers of death. This without punishment or guilt. Also, unlike the other spirits who rule over certain elements of the world and of life, they have no fixed kingdom. They go where they will and do as they please.

The magician is dependent on the good will of the Eshus to make a spell work. If he has incurred the enmity of one of these beings his efforts will fail and his luck will turn bad.

This spirit must be greeted and invoked whether he is the principle operator of the intended spell or not. Here is an example taken from the *Lucumi* tradition. As in many such invocations, the name of the spirit may be changed to the specific crossroad spirit invoked. It is not, however, a universal conjuration to be used with any spirit, but only with a representative of this class:

## INVOCATION OF ESHU

> IBARAKOU MOLLUMBA ESHU IBACO MOYUMBA IBACO MOYUMBA. OMOTE CON-ICU IBACOO OMOTE AKO MOLLUMBA ESHU KULONA. IBARAKOU MOLLUMBA OMOLE KO IBARAKOU MOLLUMVBA OMOLE KO. IBARAKOU MOLLUMBA AKO ESHU KULONA ACHE IBAKOU MOLLUMBA. ACHE ESHU KULONA IBARAKOU MOLLUMBA OMOLE KO AKO ACHE. ARONG LARO AKONG LAROLLE ESHU KULONA A ESHU COMA KOMIO ACHE. AKONKA LAR AKONKO LAR AKO ACHE IBA LA GUANA ESHU. LAROLLE AKONKO LARO LAROLLE E LAROLLE AKONKO AKNONKO LAROLLE AKONKO LAROLLE AKONKO LA GUANA E LAROLLE.

The language is corrupt *Yoruba*, called *Lucumi* in Cuba. It is easier to speak than it looks at first, since the chant is repetitive and quite musical. There are no tricks to pronunciation and the words are spoken as they appear. The "ache" referred to in the chant is the name of the primal force that is found in all magical traditions. It is the same as the "prana" of the yogis, or the "baraka" of the Arabs.

After any invocation it is customary to ask the spirit to do no harm to you or yours, and to play you no mischief in the execution of the spell. Those of you familiar with European magic will find this charge familiar.

There are several ways of representing one of these spirits during a ritual. The simplest comes from

Haiti where an equilateral cross is drawn on the floor or ground with flour, corn meal or some similar substance. This is done with various flourishes and curlicues depending on the spirit invoked or the region in which the practitioners live (see, for example, the design for the shell divination board in this book). In the United States where the Cuban form dominates, Eshu is usually called Eleggua or Elegba and is represented by a bust usually made from hand-molded concrete with eyes, ears and mouth of cowry shells. These figures are molded around a piece of doweling that is removed to leave a hollow cylindrical space in the bottom.

When *Santeria/Lucumi* was still primarily a rural practice, the head was "brought to life" by digging a hole in the center of a dirt crossroads and lowering the head into it. A rooster had its throat cut over the hole and the blood was drained into the head. The rooster was laid into this hole and buried with the bust for a prescribed number of days.

Even among the most serious practitioners, this can be impractical in a modern urban setting. An alternative, which I have followed, is to purchase an unconsecrated bust at a botanica (if there is one in your city), perform a ritual involving the above invocation, the killing of a pigeon or other easily obtainable bird over the head, allowing the blood to dry, and asking the spirit of an Eshu to

*Voodoo head used in Santeria*

indwell the head. Seven stones or coins representing the seven sacred planets of ancient astrology, as well as the African powers connected to them, are placed in the hollow space and permanently sealed up with putty or concrete. When dry, the figure should be painted black (over the dried blood), except for the shell eyes and mouth, and the figure is "charged."

These "heads" are not expensive and are usually hand-made by *Santeros* who practice in the area. The heads come in various sized from nearly that of a football to one that can fit in the palm of a hand and be easily hidden. The appropriate resting place for such a talisman is usually the corner, a cabinet, or by a door. As always, the spirit should be asked through divination what part of the house it wants to live in. A direct answer should not be disregarded. This "personal" Eshu is responsible for your personal magical rituals and the guarding of your home. It should be given candy and (if it requests them) small toys, rum and cigars. For important ceremonies Eshu prefers the fresh blood of sacrificed fowl.

As an alternative, if you live in an area where there are no botanicas and don't want to try to mold things from cement, a fresh coconut can be obtained, the "top" cut off and the liquid poured out. Shells can be glued into the "face" to represent eyes, nose, mouth and ears. Consecration can be done as above, but the seven stones should simply be dropped into the hollow interior. It need not be painted. When spells are cast requiring Eshu's help, the requests or talismans may be placed inside the hollow coconut head along with the proper rites.

In Brazil, Eshu is represented by the three-dimensional figure of a devil, often made of iron. He, or rather, they, are also represented by graphic sigils.

A selection of the literally hundreds of individuals in this family of spirits follows. Here are the twenty-one Eshus or Elegguas common in the *Santeria/Lucumi* tradition. To our knowledge these have been unpublished until recently. I obtained these names from a small booklet published by an Anglo who was initiated into the *Ifa* religion in Africa (*Esu–Elegba, Ifa and The Divine Messenger* by Awo Fa'lokun Fatunmbi, Original Publications, New York: 1992) Migene Gonzalez-Wippler has also published such a list, but the two do not match. I have selected this one partly arbitrarily and partly because of its (seeming) coherence.

**ESHU ORO**–Eshu of the power of the spoken word.
**ESHU OPIN**–The guardian of sacred space.
**ESHU ALAKETU**–Master of divine sensuality.
**ESHU ISERI**–Eshu of herbs and healing.
**ESHU GOGO**–Eshu of payment and justice.
**ESHU WARA**–Eshu of relationships.
**ESHU IJELU**–Master of the drums.
**ESHU AIYEDE**–Who brings messages from the spirits.
**ESHU ODARA**–Lord of transformation.
**ESHU JEKI EBO DA**–Eshu of sacred offerings.
**ESHU AGONGON GOJA**–Eshu of clothing or appearance.
**ESHU ELEKUN**–The hunter or predator.
**ESHU AROWOJE**–Eshu for those who travel the ocean.
**ESHU LALU**–Eshu of the dance.
**ESHU PAKUTA SI EWA**–Creator and destroyer of beauty.
**ESHU KEWE LE DUNJE**–Eshu of sweets and sweetness.
**ESHU ELEBARA**–Eshu of power.
**ESHU EMALONA**–Eshu of "any means necessary" or unusual measures.
**ESHU LAROYE**–Messenger of the love goddess Oshun.
**ESHU ANANAKI**–Eshu of remembrance of the past.
**ESHU OKOBURU**–The divine enforcer. Okoburu is *Yoruban* for "wicked cudgel."

What follows is from the truly enormous Brazilian pantheon (or demonology) of Eshu. This is a mere selection, since these spirits have been named and dealt with in the hundreds upon hundreds in *Macumba* (or *Quimbanda*, if the magic is black). The sigils that accompany them may be drawn on the ground, used as talismans, or painted large to be concentrated on like a yantra.

## ESHU REI

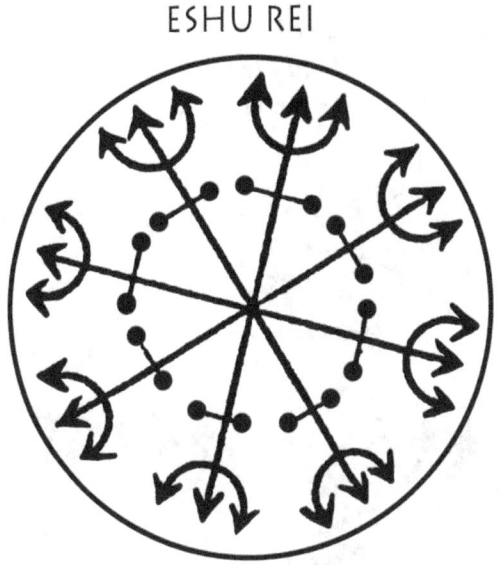

Eshu Rei, as the name suggests, is the "king Eshu," the most powerful master spirit of his class. He is to be called up only for major celebrations or operations. By reputation, if it appears at a ceremony without being called, considerable effort must be made to appease it and cause it to leave lest harm come to one and all. Conversely, if deliberately called, the reason had better be very good, and not some petty personal affair.

The safest and most beneficial way to deal with this enormous and dangerous being is to call him occasionally, offer sacrifice and ask for his general favor and that of his "family." His name can be used in invocations as a word of power to other Eshus, taking care to make it clear you are not actually calling *him*.

**Invocation:**

*Naquela encruzilhada tem um rei*
*Esse rei e seu Tranca Gira*
*Na outra encruzilhada tem outro reino*
*E do Lucifer e de Pomba Gira*

## POMBA GIRA

Pomba Gira and her sisters are the female companions or colleagues of Eshu (wife or consort would be the wrong word). Pomba Gira means "spinning pigeon" because at *Quimbanda* ceremonies where she appears, the person possessed begins the manifestation by dancing and spinning drunkenly. The character of the Pomba Giras is for the most part lascivious, promiscuous, pleasure-loving and free of all inhibitions. She has much in common with the succubus of European demonology but without the sinister overtones. I say this bearing in mind that she still has the unpredictable personality of an Eshu.

She likes alcohol and sex and both can be indulged in her honor or used as an offering. She can be used to cause the satisfaction of love, or, perhaps more appropriately, lust and vice. In a more negative sense her power can be used to cause others to lose control and disgrace or ruin themselves.

**Invocation:**
*Dona Pomba Gira e moca bonita da encruzilhada.*
*Ela vem, Ela vem, Ela vem*
*Firmar pontos na madrugada.*
*Ela deixou sua figueira*
*Tatare Eshu mulher.*
*Ela e Pomba Gira da encruza*
*A mulher de Lucifer.*

## ESHU TRANCA RUAS

Eshu Tranca Ruas specializes in aiding the magician in the blocking of the paths his enemies, or locking up their opportunities. He is to be invoked when the magician is in a competitive situation that he wishes or badly needs to win. Or when he becomes aware that someone is trying to harm him. The power of the spirit causes the

## ESHU TRANCA RUAS

focus of the spell to suffer from an inability to complete or to accomplish what he sets out to do without a hundred things going wrong.

**Invocation:**

*Essa banda e de quimbanda*
*Essa banda lhe chamou*
*Bota fogo na fundanga*
*Derruba quem demandou.*
*Eshu e coroado rei*
*Viva Eshu Tranca-Rua*
*Seu ponto e seguro na encruzilhada*
*E ganga que vem de riba*
*Firmar ponto na madrugada.*
*Eshu quer beber cachaca*
*Quer farofa na encruzilhada*
*Eshu quer ver Pomba Gira*
*Sambando na madrugada*

## ESHU MARABO

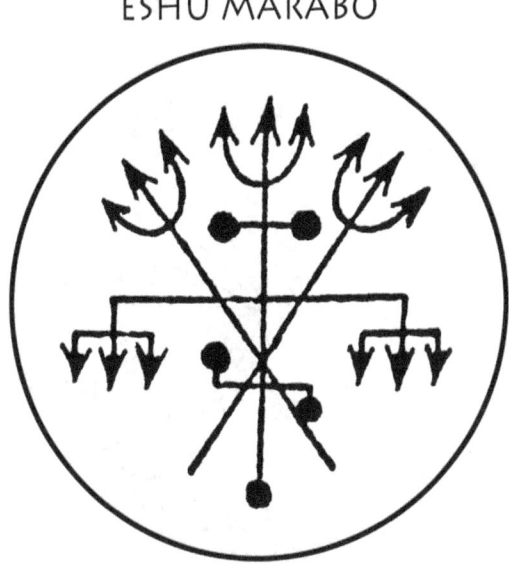

Eshu Marabo, like Eshu Tranca Ruas, is among the most "popular" of the Eshus. His power tends to be general, bringing luck or harm, with the exception of the fact that he is known to specialize in illness. Not just in terms of causing it but also of healing it. These qualities do nothing to obviate the mercurial personality of his kind, and as always, care should be taken that he is pleased with his payment.

**Invocation:**

*Poeira, poeira,*
*Poeira de Eshu Marabo, poeira*
*Poeira de Eshu Marabo, poeira*
*Poeira da encruzilhada*
*Poeira, poeira.*

## ESHU DA CAPA PRETA

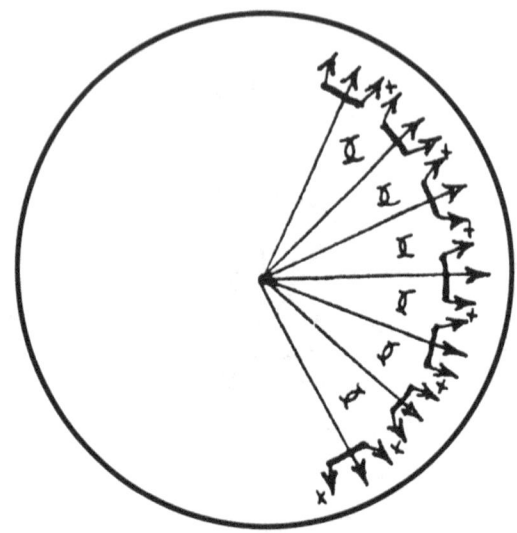

Eshu da Capa Preta is among the most sinister and dangerous of his family, specializing exclusively in the blackest magic. His name translates as "Eshu of the black cape". This conjures up images of Christopher Lee as Dracula.

Death curses, compulsions, psychic attack and spiritual slavery are all his stock in trade. Special care should be taken with the offering (use divination to find out what is desired) and with the ritual cleansing of the working space.

**Invocation:**

*Eshu da Capa Preta*
*Com ele ninguem pode*
*Tem chifres como capeta*
*E barbicha como bode.*

The invocations above are simple and should be repeated several times. In a *Macumba* ceremony they would be said or sung to the accompaniment of drums. Many of the Eshus are corrupt *Yoruban* or Congolese, and at this point all but untranslatable. The invocations themselves are far from profound in translation, their value being, like Latin or Hebrew, that they have become "sacred" and the spirits recognize them when they hear them.

For example the invocation of Eshu Marabo translates as:

*Dust, dust,*
*Dust of Eshu Marabo, dust*
*Dust of Eshu Marabo, dust*
*Dust of the crossroads*
*Dust, dust.*

*The Ibeyi, or Sacred Twins and other family members*

*Chapter 9*

# SOME OTHER MEMBERS OF THE FAMILY

The following are descriptions and sigils of many of the *Orishas* invoked in *Lucumi* and *Macumba*. The sigils are almost all Brazilian as this particular form of express did not find fertile ground in Cuba. Bear in mind that each of the spirits, like the Eshus, have many "paths" or as I have put it, "members" of their family. If some variation of the classical description of the spirit appears, it does not imply failure or a mistake. You may have simply contacted one of the many "Changos" or "Oshuns".

## THE IBEYI, OR SACRED TWINS: TAEBO AND KAINDE

Taebo and Kainde are the twin sons of Chango (the thunder god) and Oshun (the equivalent of Venus) whose descriptions follow. The twins are perpetually youthful, intelligent, playful and excellent at solving problems. They are particularly talented at curing illness, most particularly mental or emotional illness.

Taebo and Kainde are also good at causing luck at gambling, until they get bored, and are often appealed to in a situation where a "miracle" is needed. In such a situation, the supplicant creates an altar to the twins, with either the figures of two identical boys or a picture of St. Cosmo and St. Damain. Then a "party" is thrown in their honor, with cake, ice cream and anything else that children would like. This can take the form of an actual party with others guests if appropriate. If they are happy with the party, the miracle will occur.

It is appropriate to offer a blood sacrifice only if it is specifically requested. The correct offerings are usually identical plates of sweets or cakes left before their images or talisman.

Their colors are those of their parents, Chango and Oshun.

**Invocation:**

*Vamos comer caruru, dois, dois.*
*Na praia tem carura.*
*Vamos comer caruru, dois, dois.*
*No bosque tem caruru.*
*Vamos comer caruru, dois, dois.*
*No terreiro tem carurua.*
*Vamos comer munguaza*
*Vamos chamar as criancas*
*Pra Sarava no conga.*
*Vamos chamar o Joaozinho*
*Mariazinha e Cipriano*
*Vamos chamar o Zezinho*
*O Manezinho e o Mariano*

## CHANGO

This most masculine and macho of spirits has been rather hilariously masked as the ethereal and feminine St. Barbara. This occurred simply because of the presence of

Chango's symbols in her picture, just as St. Patrick became the mask of Dambalah in Haiti for no other reason than that there were snakes in the picture. His traditional image is that of a beautiful, very muscular man who carries a double-headed ax.

His colors are red and white and his day is Friday.

Chango is possibly the most popular of all the spirits and he is worshipped under the same name and with the same attributes from Los Angeles to Haiti. He can bring luck, love, strength (physical and moral) and sexual prowess. He likes to get drunk, but sometimes forbids his followers to do the same. He is also a womanizer and a talented magician hence his usefulness in love spells. He is a lord of thunder and fire and can cause storms and tempests.

His usual offerings include the sweetest, reddest apples that can be found, pomegranates and palm oil. Among the birds he prefers as blood offerings are roosters, and quail. He also accepts turtles.

**Invocation:**

*Abrindo a minha engira*
*Com Zambi e com Chango!*
*Abrindo a minha engira*
*Com Zambi e com Chango!*
*Sarava, seu Alafim!*
*Sarava, seu Algoao!*
*Sarava, seu Alafim!*
*Sarava, seu Alganju!*

## OSHUN

Oshun is the love goddess of the *Yorubas* and the patroness of gold. She is the mother of the Ibeyi twins and, because of her attributes, one of the most popular spirits. She is invoked in love spells, particularly by women, and by men in the acquisition of wealth. It is said that she is moody, and must be kept satisfied, or she will take away all she has given. If you have made a promise to her and do not keep it, you can make no greater enemy.

She also has power over that part of the human anatomy where the stomach, digestive tract and reproductive organs are located, thus, she is also appealed to in matters of fertility and any ailments of the stomach or colon.

Her colors are white and yellow, her day is Saturday, and her mask is the Virgin of Caridad del Cobre, the patroness of Cuba.

Her sacred place in nature, aside from the bedroom, is around fresh flowing water, such as rivers and streams. Offerings or spells done in her honor are especially effective if done at a river or stream. These should not be done by the ocean, as that is the kingdom of her sister Yemanja.

She is envisioned as a beautiful woman with copper-colored skin and long hair. Along with gold, her sacred metal is copper (which was also sacred to the Greek Venus).

**Invocation:**

*Mamae Oshun*
*Papai Ogum Beira Mar*
*Estavam brincando na areia*
*Com o rosario de Iemanja*
*Arue minha mae*
*Minha mae me ensinou a nadar*
*Minha mae e raihna do mar*
*Tem areia, Tem areia*
*Adociaba no mar*
*Mamae Sereia.*

OGUN

Ogun is the fighter-god, the war-god. He is lord of iron and patron of all conflicts and competitions. His mask is usually St. Peter (in Brazil it is St. George) and his day is Tuesday. He is lord of tools and weapons such as machetes and hammers.

His colors are green and black. For ordinary offerings he is fond of cigars and rum and his altar is decorated with miniature weapons and tools that are sold in most botanicas. In Brazil he is often portrayed as a roman soldier, and some similar figure would be an appropriate altar piece.

He is called upon to gain work for any matter regarding stone, metal or heavy machinery. He safeguards from accidents and like all spirits can also operate negatively in any of these areas.

**Invocation:**

*Ogun, Ogun, de Timbire*
*Ogun de mana Zambe dao Luanda*
*As aves cantam quando ele vem de Aruanda*
*Trazendo pembra para salvar filhos de Unbanda*
*Oh japones, olha as costas do mar*
*Oh japones, olha as costas do mar.*

## OCHOSI, THE HUNTER

Ochosi is patron of hunters, birds and wild animals. He and his fellow hunter spirits are vital to any culture that lives off the land, and his like can be found the world over. In Brazil, figures of various Ochosis look like native Indians, with steady eye and bow in hand. He is patron of hunters, birds and wild animals. His colors are violet, red, green and blue.

## OCHOSI, THE HUNTER

He is the leader of the "caboclos" or Indian spirits. In Voodoo the native elementals and the spirits of dead Indians are evoked as allies. This phenomenon even occurred in white American society during the advent of Spiritualism, when a number of famous mediums had "red Indians" as their spirit guides.

He has a number of masks, but our favorite is the one used in Brazil: St. Sebastian. Whether in the form of a statue or a print, Sebastian presents a wonderfully macabre figure, and demonstrates the frequent irony that the Catholic "mask" presents, since the arrows are *in* him rather than being shot *by* him. Stamped metal charms depicting a bow and arrow can be purchased at botanicas and carried as a talisman.

His offerings are toasted corn, palm oil, all game fowl and corn meal.

With his arrow representing the element of air, he is called upon magically to gain alertness and perception, to triumph in legal situations and to send an "arrow" of psychic force against enemies. As a hunter he aids in finding things lost, stolen, or desired.

**Invocation:**
*Eu tenho tres flechas*
*Tres flechas de guine*
*Uma e de Ochosi*
*Outra e de guine*
*E outra e pra quem quiser.*

## YEMANJA

Yemanja is the sea goddess. She is patroness of fertility and the abundance of life. In *Lucumi*, she is masked by Our Lady of Regla, but in Brazil where these spirits

*Statue of Yemanja*

are far more publicly represented, she is pictured in statues and prints as either a mermaid or a woman dressed in pearls and blue robes.

Her colors are blue and white in *Lucumi* and crystal in *Macumba*. As offerings she accepts many types of fruits, especially watermelon. For animal offerings, pigeons and live fish and crustaceans are most obtainable.

In magic, she is called upon regarding any problem regarding the ocean and can give great wealth from the sea, protecting those who work on it. She is the ruler of all woman's affairs and is patroness of women in general. She is also associated with the moon and has the attributes and gives the gifts common to moon goddesses.

*Voodoo practitioners celebrating Yemanja by the sea.*

## Invocation:

*Sou filho do mar.*
*Das ondas do mar*
*Da espuma do mar*
*Minlia mae Yemanja*
*O, Virgem Maria*
*Como es linda flor,*
*Celeste harmonia,*
*Dulcissimo amor.*
*Manda em nossos lares*
*Rinha dos mares,*
*Da Terra e dos Ceus,*
*Em risos encobres.*
*Maria os seus dons,*
*Tesouro dos pogres*
*Riqueza do bons.*
*Manda em nossos lares*
*Rainha dos mares,*
*Da Terra o dos Ceus.*

*Fabric bags hold herbs and incense and are placed on the altar.*

*Chapter 10*
# COCAINE, ZOMBIES & CAULDRONS OF BLOOD

In nearly every recent account by sympathetic writers about Voodoo–whether Haitian or Cuban or Brazilian–great effort is made to point out that uninformed accounts of the subject malign it and the people who practice it. They say that the tales of altars running with blood and the casting of curses are the sensational accounts of ignorant journalists or religious bigots.

This is usually true. It is also true that these same books often end with tales of the very things they seek to play down. Like a priest's fondness for schoolboys or proliferation of fundamentalist mental clinics, it's one of those things that is hard to completely ignore.

Most Americans have memories long enough to recall the invasion of Panama that garnered General Noriega's company in a federal prison. What most of us did not notice, because the various media covered it only fleetingly, was what the military discovered in the General's mansion after making the arrest.

When the army entered the house to collect evidence they found a large room dominated by a long table covered with glass-encased candles, strange statues, and little cloth bags among other obscure items. The bags were found to contain powder of various kinds and so they were taken for examination under the assumption that they were drugs. When analyzed, the powder was found to be an inert (from their point of view) mixture of herbs and incenses. The matter was largely forgotten, thought it came out later that the General had, in his employ, one or more sorcerers of Brazilian, Cuban or Puerto Rican provenance.

The use of magic to attain and maintain power is not unusual. Americans know very little about it only because most journalists consider it irrelevant or are so ignorant they don't know what they are looking at when they see it. One of the recent presidents of Brazil (at least!) is said to have been a devotee of *Quimbanda*; and the Duvaliers of Haiti are well known to have practiced the black side of Voodoo and to have made alliances with its secret societies.

Related to the above, I have a story to relate told to me by a psychologist friend who went to Brazil just after "Baby Dock" Duvalier fled Port au Prince. He told me that the former members of the notorious *tonton macoute* had found a welcome haven in some parts of Brazil. Their off-shore bank accounts no doubt helped. At any rate, he swore to me that he had seen numbers of people who had crossed them, or been poor workers in their employ (he didn't inquire too closely) in the "zombie" condition. The toxic formula described by Wade Davis in his book had been used on these people as was a formula of magical mind programming. He told me that he saw these people daily, carrying burdens (it was a rural area) or just standing around, utterly gone.

No secret was made of what had happened to these people, as it enhanced the prestige of the former enforcers and saved them the trouble of having to do it to too many others. I have never seen this story confirmed in any article or media report, nor would I particularly expect to. I have it from the person who claimed he saw it, and beyond that, I have no proof except that in many parts of the world, such a thing is far from unusual.

The late unlamented Idi Amin of Uganda was also known to have extensively employed black magicians. This was far more widely reported because ritual cannibalism was involved.

I have read a published account by a supposed witness who claims that Amin abducted someone who had offended him and that one of the most powerful and popular sorcerers-for-hire in Africa strapped him to a table and slowly skinned him alive during a ritual to capture his soul as a slave for Mr. Amin. His body was mummified and kept in a chest as the "link" to imprison his soul.

The immediate reaction by most people is that the above is the most scurrilous and ridiculous kind of rumor. I do not know if this particular story is absolutely true. What I *do* know is that what I described is a genuine part of traditional African black magic that is practiced to this day. In fact, a little more than a year ago, television network news reported that helpless refugees from one of the African nations were being abducted and killed in just such ceremonies.

Not long ago, also nationally reported, the family of a Brazilian mayor was nearly lynched by a mob when it was discovered that they were part of a black magic circle responsible for the torture murder of a number of young children (probably by skinning, but they tried to keep the details quiet) and whose heads were then kept in cauldrons for use in magic.

And this brings us to the world of *Palo Mayombe*.

*Palo Mayombe* (or *Palo Monte*) is magic that has its roots in the Congo region just as *Lucumi* is basically *Yoruban* and Haitian *Vaudun* is basically Dahomean. It is by no means always black, but it always involves the remains of the dead, as it is beyond anything else, a technique of necromancy. Its initiated practitioners are called *Paleros* or *Tata N'kisi* (which means father of the spirits.

In Cuba, an elaborate initiation ceremony is performed wherein the aspiring sorcerer sleeps out of doors for a night and then digs up a corpse from a graveyard. The skull, flanges of the fingers, and tibia are removed and taken away to a ceremonial chamber where the spirit of the dead person is conjured.

I will not go into metaphysical speculation on whether a human soul can be bound after death.

If the spirit consents to serve the magician during his lifetime, a container is prepared for the human remains to serve as a "home." This is usually an iron cauldron filled with a bed of graveyard earth and other ingredients upon which the skull and other bones rest. "Primitive" as this sounds, the details of the arrangement make it clear that within the cauldron is created a microcosmic universe that could have been understood and appreciated by any renaissance hermeticist. This cauldron is called either a *nganga*, from the African, or a *prenda*, which is Spanish for "jewel", representing how precious it is.

*Palo Mayombe* is a complex and time-honored system of magic, and I would like to emphasize that the vast majority of *Paleros* absolutely do NOT participate in the kind of atrocity that I am about to describe.

Nearly ten years ago, a boy from Texas disappeared during a weekend drinking trip to Matamoros, Mexico with some of his college buddies. As a result of the search that followed, a mass grave was uncovered at an isolated ranch outside of town. The boy's body was there, as were many others. Eventually, the story came out that many years, a powerful *Palero* from Florida had been working for the local drug-running families providing not only magical protection, but organizational services as well.

His name was Adolfo Luis Constanzo, and his full story is told in a fascinating book called *Buried Secrets* by Pulitzer prize winning author Edward Humes (Signet, New York: 1992). He was (according to himself) an initiated *Palero* of Cuban extraction who had been trained in blood magic since he was a child. This fantastic personality was personal advisor to some of Mexico's most famous and powerful people, from movie stars to high-level politicians.

He was also a monster who routinely skinned people alive on an altar in order to feed the spirit servitor in his bloody *nganga* pot. I've read several accounts of him and every author says repeatedly that the people who knew him insist that his spells "worked." What he foretold came to pass. If he did a spell for luck, your fortunes skyrocketed. Mr. Humes is a highly respected journalist, not a writer on "the strange world of psychic phenomena" yet he was clearly impressed by the consistency of these stories.

It becomes clear that Constanzo was a genuine psychic prodigy who was born into an environment where such talent could be focused and trained properly, and he used that ability like the sorcerers of old–to gain wealth and power. What was uncovered when he made the mistake of killing an American was a public horror, but what was even worse is the clear conclusion that if it was not for that error in judgment he might never have been caught or interfered with. He was almost a modern Gilles de Rais. It is amusing to compare the "magicians" and "witches" of American occult lodges with this powerful and wealthy monster.

In Florida, which has been the focus for the influx of Voodoo practitioners of all types, the police deal routinely with the involvement of professional black magicians in the drug trade. In Miami, gangland "hits" are often accompanied by *Vaudun* or *Lucumi* signs near the body. This is not to say that they were human sacrifices. They were the victims of crime rivalry with the added spice of having their souls captured or meddled with as additional punishment. *Paleros* and *Santeros* also do a heavy trade providing spiritual "luck" for cocaine traffickers.

It may surprise you that the fear of the werewolf is still very much a part of the modern world. The explorer and documentary film-maker Douchan Gersi in his book *Faces In The Smoke* (Jeremy P. Parcher, Los Angeles: 1991) relates how he interviewed a number of people including military men who swore that they had caught and killed a lycanthrope that had been terrorizing the countryside. They told the classic story that when they cornered the beast it was in the form of a monster, but after death reverted to a man. Whatever the truth of the story, Mr. Gersi said that the wounds were real and the deaths caused by the "beast" were real. And on top of that he saw the corpse of the accused lycanthrope.

In Cuba, South America, Mexico and some parts of the southwestern U.S. this rumor still persists, with multiple witnesses and sometimes injuries and death to indicate that *something* happened. Those who are prepared to accept the efficacy of a spell or the operation of telepathy may draw the line at shape-shifting, but it is far better attested to than you might think. Most accounts indicate that the "wolf" isn't real, but an apparition that is nevertheless capable of doing harm. The sorcerer is often in a trance of some kind miles away, his spirit only in animal form. The writings of Carlos Castaneda also touch on this sort of thing.

The world is not what we are taught it is, and when the veil is pulled aside it can be weirder and more dangerous than anyone is willing to believe.

*Agua Florida*

*Chapter 11*
# SPELLS

In this chapter I create a basic outline for the practical working of spells in the Voodoo tradition. Those familiar with the literature of magic will find that the basic ingredients and techniques are very little different from European witchcraft.

As this is intended to be a book that introduces outsiders to the practice of Afro-Caribbean magic, I will avoid much that is culturally specific or initially obscure. For example, the tradition of herbalism in all forms of Voodoo is truly enormous, and the majority of it is still passed along only by word of mouth. As an added complication, the names used for the herbs are different than those commonly used in the U.S., even when the names are in English.

Also note that there is no particular separation between, day, a Haitian technique or one of *Lucumi* origin. In New York and Florida, for example, there are Haitian immigrants who are initiates into *Santeria*, and *Santeros* who are also *Paleros*. Voodoo is about function and not artificial divisions based on meaningless sectarian symbolism. This, from our experience, seems to be one of the hardest things for people raised in a white Christian world to get past.

No *Bocor* or *Palero* would hesitate to use material from the *Key of Solomon* or any other European Grimoire if he thought it would work, and I urge you to take the same attitude. In this sense the Voodoo practitioner is the ultimate pragmatist.

While the principle focus of the book has been on spirit names of a Yoruban origin, there is no need to limit yourself to this.

The symbols used on the "board" created for the shell divination are Haitian. The symbol for Legba is related to the family of the Eshus, the symbol of Erzulie is related to Oshun, the symbol of Baron Samedi represents a spirit like Eshu Da Capa Preta and Erzulie Dantor is sister to Pomba Gira. Both Chango and Ogun are worshipped under the same names and qualities.

To begin with, like all basic magic, these spells operate under the concept that what is similar to the mind or senses is similar in reality. This idea, ancient beyond calculation is the basis for the "doctrine of signatures" espoused by the Hermetic magicians and physicians of Europe.

## The Spell of Attraction

First, it is important to create a link between the spell or force you are creating and its object or target. The closer the better. First in effectiveness are effluvia from the body itself; second, an object or article of clothing that the target has owned and carried for a long time; third a piece of writing or a signature and finally, a picture or simply an image in your mind.

Assuming that you have some sort of physical link–even a picture–take a container that is large enough to hold this link and place the object inside it. Along with this place a lodestone (commonly available at botanicas) or a small magnet that you can buy at any toy store. Cover these with honey. Next, invoke one of the lords of the crossroads and ask for help in contacting the forces necessary to make the spell work.

Light a candle by the container and call upon the spirit to help in this operation. Take care that a proper offering is made. Always take the trouble to verbalize exactly what you want–and, if appropriate, why you want it–as though you were speaking to a person present in the room with you. Do not assume that the spirit is reading your mind.

Repeat this process for at least five days in a row, leaving the candle burning while you are in the house.

**Another Spell of Attraction**

Similar to the above, but simpler, is to write the name of the desired lover on a piece of paper, and place it in a dish. Cover with honey or syrum while invoking Oshun and lighting a candle in her honor. Ideally the candle should be allowed to burn completely out, but if this is a safety hazare, keep it burning while you are at home. Don't blow the candle out. Snuff it out.

**Another Spell of Attraction**

This spell is particularly useful in difficult cases, where you may want the love or good graces of someone who is unlikely to give it. Call on the Ibeyi twins, Taebo and Kainde, and offer them cakes and cookies. Talk to them of your problem and give them the name and description of the person to be influenced. Wait at least a day. Then take a small portion of the sweets and crumble it into a powder. Place this on the floor or pathway that the target of the spell must walk over, or hide it someplace where they spend time.

### A Spell of Attraction, Lust or Control

As described in the chapter on Eshu, obtain a fresh coconut, cut an opening in it, and remove the liquid. Glue shells to one side to create a face, or if these are unavailable use paint. Place the name and/or picture of the object of the spell within the hollow figure, and call upon the proper Eshu.

The spirit must be offered rum, candy and cigars. If the spell is particularly serious, the offering of a bird such as a pigeon may be made.

Broadly speaking, this spell may be used for any purpose regarding the influence or control of another, whether for love, lust, or defeat, all depending on the nature of the Eshu conjured. With this, as with other spells, time should be devoted to it. A candle should be burned by the figure and the conjuration and request made each night or day for a week or even longer.

### To Cause Dissension

Basically the same as the above, except that you need links for the two people whom you wish to cause a falling out. Place them in the container and cover with vinegar instead of honey, and call upon one of the more violent spirits, such as Eshu Da Capa Preta.

## To Block Someone's Path

Take a black candle, preferably molded in the shape of a person and carve the name of the target of the spell upon it. Call upon Eshu Da Capa Petra and say that you give this person to him, that all of his affairs will fail and his efforts come to nothing. Explain to the spirit why this should be so, and do not question or qualify what may happen to the target. Release the spirit to take his pleasure upon this person and light the candle. Let it burn down, but save the remaining wax, either keeping it in your freezer as a magical imprisonment of his spirit, or burying it in a cemetery, leaving a small bottle of rum hidden as payment to the spirits of the graveyard.

## To Remove or Destroy an Enemy

Make or obtain a cloth Voodoo doll. Open it, and place within it a parchment with the person's name, as well as any magical link with the person that you might have. On top of this, sprinkle cayenne pepper, asafoetida, and (if you can get them) stinging nettles. If you wish you may also place the body of a wasp or scorpion inside. The doll should then be sewn up.

Select the appropriate spirit and call upon it to bring destruction upon or to remove the person. You may bind the doll with cord and keep it in a symbolic prison in your home, or you may hide or bury the doll in or near where the object of the curse works or lives. As a third alternative, it may be buried in a cemetery with a gift of rum for the graveyard spirits.

## For Destruction of an Enemy

Construct a miniature coffin of either cardboard or wood. Buy or construct a doll of way, clay or cloth and unit it with a physical link belonging to the target. Place them in the coffin. Baptize the doll in the name of the person to whom you desire to do harm.

Call upon a death spirit such as Eshu Da Capa Preta or Baron Samedi and perform an impromptu funeral over the doll. At no time refer to it in any way other than as the person you wish to destroy. NEVER call it "the doll." Do this for three days in succession taking care to make the "funeral" as convincing as possible. At the end of the three days either bury the coffin (preferably in a cemetery) or cremate it. Expect results within a month. Remember, doing spells such as these are not actionable in U.S. courts.

**To Cause an Enemy to Depart**

Obtain a quantity of graveyard earth, call upon the spirit you think is most appropriate and explain in detail why this person should be removed from your vicinity. Create a small shrine with a candle and an offering to the spirit. During the invocation, the graveyard earth should be "charged" with power.

The earth should be powdered finely and scattered over an area where the person is sure to walk. This can be either in or out of doors. The operation should be repeated for at least a week if practical and invocations for the desired effect done each night.

**For Money and Prosperity**

Perform an invocation of Oshun. Use her colors (see the chapter on the spirits) and if possible candles with a picture of La Caridad Del Cobre, her Catholic mask. These are available at botanicas and many religious supply stores. Otherwise use green candles and anoint them with the money-drawing oil that can be obtained at any botanica or occult shop.

Place an appropriate offering to Oshun on a plate before the candles, and tell her of your needs and desires. Take a piece of silver or gold, or even a dollar, and anoint it with the money-draw oil. Place this in an envelope or mojo bag and carry it with you. Light the candles and say the invocation every night for at least a week and you will see your luck change.

**For Prosperity**

Select the appropriate spirit. Take a sum of money, preferably genuine silver (not the rubbish minted nowadays) or a piece of quality jewelry. Pour the blood of a sacrifice on the object in the name of the spirit, and place some of the blood on a talisman inscribed with the sign of the spirit. Carry the talisman on your person, and perform the invocation to the spirit at least three nights a week.

**For a Cleansing**

This is done to rid yourself of bad luck or bad feelings. Cleanse the room in which you sleep by splashing the four quarters of the floor with "Florida water"–a mild, citrus smelling cologne that is available in botanicas and stores catering to a Latin clientele. It will not stain, and the clean, pleasant smell will soon evaporate. If this substance is not available, use incense or another cologne of your choice. The Native American incense sage has also recently become widely available, and is traditionally used for this purpose.

Take either a live pigeon (If you consider this matter serious) or two eggs. Pass these over your body from your feet, over your head, down to the other side, and up and down the back and front of your torso. As you do this, ask the spirits to take the impurities from your spiritual and physical body. Then kill the bird by breaking its neck (do not cut its throat) and place it in a plain paper bag–or place the eggs in a paper bag with six pennies. Leave the bag at the corner of an intersection, unobtrusively against a building.

**A Lesser Cleansing and Spell of Protection**

This is done in the name of Legba, Eleggua or one of the Eshus. Take a figure or sign of one of these beings–Legba's cross for example–and place it prominently in the place you wish to protect. Obtain a bottle of Florida Water or even holy water from a Catholic church. Perform the invocation to Eshu. Then, take the bottle of liquid and go around the space to be cleansed, sprinkling the substance very liberally. While doing this, visualize a barrier of white light blocking the entrance of all destructive influences and calling upon the spirits of the crossroads to guard you and reserve their mischief only for those persons or things that would cause you harm.

All of these spells are only simple outlines that can be expanded to much more elaborate versions. The most important element in this form of magic is direct communication with the spirit world, hence the emphasis earlier on various means of divination. Once these techniques are mastered, direct communication should provide you with instruction from the disembodied intelligences themselves, and you can dispense with the basic methods.

*Chapter 12*
# INITIATION & SELF-INITIATION

An important question regarding the practice of Voodoo and *Santeria* is the question of initiation. From our experience it is not easy for a person raised outside these traditions to become an *official* practitioner of either. This raises serious questions about the efficacy and safety of practice. Some theorists believe that one should only follow one's own tradition although one might *experiment* with other traditions. This last argument is very weak and reflects more a need for uniformity and stability than for safety and effectiveness.

I have been initiated into a number of esoteric groups which claim to practice magic. I've experimented within these groups and observed their traditions. Much of what is practiced there is an amalgam of many other traditions. Simply put, I've never been initiated into a Wicca group, yet I sometimes practice rituals which are similar to Wicca in my work.

The prime example is the Hermetic Order of the Golden Dawn which is regarded by some as the pinnacle of Western Esoteric Magic.

The first question to consider: is the Golden Dawn an original system–a thing in itself? The answer is "no." It, too, is an amalgam of numerous traditions, including Greek, Roman, Egyptian, Hebrew, and Christian.

*The Hermetic Order of the Golden Dawn*

The followers of the Golden Dawn attempt to defend it against the claim of being an amalgam of other traditions and systems by invoking its jewel, Enochiana, which was "channeled" by Mr. Kelly to Dr. Dee. This notion in and of itself is open to numerous questions and has been a topic of heated debate for many decades.

Regardless of the authenticity of the Enochian system, the entire history of the Golden Dawn is filled with forgery and fraud. This is true for many other systems as well. Entire books have been written from falsified papers, channeled "secrets" and by false prophets.

Even today many of the heads of various Golden Dawn Temples claim that they are the only legitimate "heirs." Of what one may ask? An illegitimate Order to begin with? However, with all this aside, the Golden Dawn itself is a workable system. If used properly it can help a student learn magic and aid him in his spiritual and personal development.

I have known hundreds of people who have been initiated into the Golden Dawn system. The authenticity of each initiation can be questioned because, as stated above, the origins of the Golden Dawn itself are questionable. More important than the "papers" each person holds are the results he or she has obtained. On this topic I have much less information.

If the Golden Dawn survives another few hundred years, new wonder stories will be created and the actual history will be ignored, much as the history of the Catholic Church is ignored. The same thing has happened with other forms of Christianity. Luther's illumination is sufficient as the inspirational component, and time has done the rest to make it legitimate. Often the proof of legitimacy–other than power and violence–is how long something has survived. The longer something has been around and is still functional, the more legitimate and holy it becomes. Our short life span makes it easy to fool us into believing things that are false. This is the major purpose of history–to time-bind events for the future from the perspective of the historian.

The question remains: are those individuals "formally" initiated into the Golden Dawn any better at what they do than someone who has practiced the work and forgone the initiation? In this context the term "better" simply means "effective." I don't have the answer. I doubt that they are any "worse." But there is no doubt that some believe that without the link to the hidden masters–given in practice by pompous fools–the magic of the uninitiated is either evil or impotent.

Initiation implies a link with the etheric forces of an Order which is supposed to provide power and protection from otherwise dangerous forces. This is based on the assumption that the forces will recognize you if you possess the link. If the link is missing it is assumed that the practitioner, no matter how powerful, can get himself into trouble and is regarded as inauthentic, heretic and an outsider. Often the real purpose of initiation is to get the individual to believe in the wonder stories about the organization. It is often used just as it is in Christianity– as indoctrination. Step by step, grade by grade, in theory you are becoming more powerful, but ironically less dangerous to the Order's hierarchical structure.

There is no doubt that mistakes can be avoided by following the tried and true path. There is also no doubt that rarely is anything new or better created by following the tried and true path. The etheric question is on issue that can't easily be glossed over. Israel Regardie, one of the foremost experts in the field, felt that a properly done self-initiation was an adequate alternative to initiation by a group of individuals who had the "proper papers." Why?

Regardie said:

> In stating that the isolated student could now be his own initiator, one important phrase is rendered imperative. And that is he must be persistent and as thoroughgoing and exacting as if he were an initiator in a regularly constituted Golden Dawn temple under the constant scrutiny of officialdom and higher adept authorities. The responsibility for progress is

thus placed inexorably on the student or candidate himself. As I see it–and I have watched this on a very few students–each elemental initiation or Watchtower ceremony requires its repetition several times. One student whom I am thinking of at this juncture has performed the whole...ceremonies some 50 or 60 times. It is therefore my opinion that she has initiated herself as effectively and as positively as any temple initiatory hierophantic team could possible do.[1]

The idea of degrees or papers must be kept separate from the issue of competency. I have known psychotherapists with no credentials who were more capable than most men of "letters." Credentials, however, do provide the sanction of the powers who have the authority to issue them which, for most people, is more important than competency.

The need for legitimacy is reflected in the maneuvers the founders of the Golden Dawn went through to create for themselves the correct papers to substantiate their wonder stories. (See *What You Should Know About The Golden Dawn*, New Falcon Publications, 2020).

Dr. Regardie had another point regarding self-initiation. He felt that some people are "called" to certain traditions. This can happen by "accident", or through a dream, a vision, a possession or an array of other "coincidences." In Regardie's discussion of self-initiation into Neophyte grade of the Golden Dawn he concluded that,

---

[1] *The Complete Golden Dawn System of Magic*, New Falcon Publications, 1984, Vol. 1, p. 9.

Dr. Israel Regardie

...initiation outside of a regularly constituted Temple was only possible with two students. They would have to prove to themselves–not to anyone else–that they were wholly devoted to the Great Work, devoted enough to spend at least several months jointly or individually practising the Middle Pillar...

Dr. Regardie continues by emphasizing.

...If this practice were assiduous and intense both students would have awakened in themselves the psycho-spiritual energy that could not only hasten their own inner development but that the latter could be communicated to yet another in a manner not too dissimilar to that described in Z-3.

The fundamental requirement was that the initiator should be an initiator–not a layman out of the brute herd. Something must have happened to him or have redeemed him of the stigma of being 'ordinary.' Of course it would have been better if he (or she) had been the recipient of a spontaneous mystical experience of the type described in James...Since this kind of attainment cannot be made to order, as it were, the only alternative is to fall back on time honored methods of development and growth.[1]

---

[1] *Op. cit.*, pp. 10-11.

I've had numerous mystical experiences and, combined with my own personal workings, feel that I meet the criterion laid down by Dr. Regardie at least in terms of the practice of Voodoo so as not to deceive myself or anyone else. I have twenty-five years of practice in the Western Esoteric tradition and my style of Voodoo reflects my origins and experiences.

Sometimes special people can't receive initiation or do not want to because of their intense natures. They are rogues who must go it on their own. Others find initiation very difficult. They do not like groups or attending meetings. This means, they, too, go it alone. They buy books, study, practice, make mistakes, innovate and come up with their own system. Between the good material available today, and other rogues with whom to share experiences and learn, it is not necessary to seek organized forms of initiation. While I have taken the route of the rogue in some instances, in other cases I have gone through normal process of initiation. There were many reasons behind taking formal initiations. In one case it was out of respect for my teacher; in others it was to see what was behind the veil. Unfortunately, more often than not, there was nothing.

One problem with "the going it alone route": if you later require acknowledgment of your expertise from a groups, you will rarely get it even if you are really good– and sometimes because you are *too* good. If you do receive some acceptance, may be treated as an outsider, unless of course you are so powerful you can "storm the temple" and take it over.

Some groups, particularly when they are starting up, will accept degrees or levels of initiation from other groups. This is rare and still requires some sort of initiation into the new group.

Insiders and outsiders have always been an important issue for anthropologists and sociologists. Usually they attempt to interpret these issues in a utilitarian fashion. Often, they miss the point.

Outsiders have always been the innovators, the creators of new systems and the rejuvenators of older systems. Every successful rebel becomes the new dictator who later is overcome by new and more vibrant forces.

If one chooses to become initiated into an "alien" tradition, he will by necessity have to go through the ordeals set by his teachers. I have done it in many ways. I have had traditional initiations, semi-traditional initiations and none at all. One effect of traditional initiation is the imprint created in the mind. For me this had lasting importance in some cases, but so did my first love affair. I have created similar effects on my own or with a few associates who I trusted.

Being a legitimate member of a group allows one to feel superior to outsiders as well as to climb the hierarchy by passing exams, biding one's time and being in favor with the authorities.

In Voodoo, however, results achieved by reputation are more important than "passing exams" and attending empty formalities. The same holds true for those who are unfortunately called "fortune tellers." Reputation and results can often override degrees, diplomas or initiations.

What is important is integrity, a sense of calling, and lots of practice—which, of course, implies lots of mistakes. Knowing when you made a mistake is much harder to determine in the practice of magic than in surgery. Sometimes the results you want from a magical operation bring a lot of discomfort and anxiety. Things might well work out in the end, but the process of getting there can at least be said to be exciting. I have had numerous experiences which seem to indicate that I had made an error but after a period of discomfort which often motivated me further I have more often than not found out that I was on the right path after all.

The practice of Voodoo demands that a person own his actions. This is no different from the performance of any type of *real* magic. The concept of personal responsibility is particularly true when the practitioner does not belong to a community—it is easy to blame the group or the teacher. This aside, the solitary practitioner must alone decide on the value of his rituals and actions. There is no community, no priest, no doctor or official.

For many modern men this is horrifying since they are used to hiring priests and others, not only to do their work for them, but to blame for their own disowned desires.

For example: a greedy man wants more money, so he hires a broker but the broker fails. The rage aimed at the broker not only for his failure but because of he man's own greed. The motive becomes intertwined with the methods designed to satisfy the greed. The result is to blame the broker.

The same is true when we refuse to take responsibility for revenge. A person with integrity doesn't take revenge on the beautiful simply because he is less beautiful. One must have the utmost integrity to take revenge in a constructive way. If you are unhappy because of what you are, change, or learn to transform yourself. Don't blame a better man for your weakness. Blame instead the slave mentality which permeates the entire world.

## A Method of Self-Initiation

For a person who wishes to practice Voodoo and doesn't want initiation or can't find a suitable means I present a method which works. Keep in mind that you must decide what you can or can't tolerate. Only you are responsible for what you chose to do. You paid for this book–as such you paid for my experiences and knowledge. What you do with this book is up to you–it is your responsibility. Remember, even though there are millions of people who follow Voodoo, this is no justification for irresponsible actions. You must decide how serious you are and how much suffering you might be willing to tolerate.

An intensive set of divinations are first necessary. Obtain equipment, buy an image, set up a circle, prepare an altar, perform a sacrifice, purify yourself, play music, listen to sounds, choose colors, prepare a talisman, perform a ritual at least once a week for a month. Pay attention to dreams, coincidences, etc.

Keep a journal of your practices.

Without benefit of a "real" *Santero* or *Houngan* to initiate you, there is another tradition of far greater age that can be adapted to the purpose for the serious student.

According to shamanic lore, a person who has reason to believe that they has been "called" to the practice of magic often goes into the forest by himself and, by use of spontaneous trance states, learns the arts of magic from the spirits themselves. In other words, they go off by themselves in a state of ignorance and return with a body of knowledge obtained from persons or things unknown. Parallels to this exist in every religious tradition including the Christian.

For many, going on a pilgrimage into the forest may be inconvenient, so I have here a simple method based on tradition. Its principle requirements are a commitment of time and a serious willingness to a rather scary form of psychic openness.

For this you will need a very simple devotional space or altar. You will also need some form of crossroad spirit like an Eleggua who will be the person you will principally address.

You should cover this space with a white cloth and have at least one glass-encased candle and perfumed oil or Florida water to anoint the figure or sigil.

This exercise should be done both morning and evening. Begin with a ritual bath or washing. When the water is drawn, say this over it:

LORD GOD ADONAY, WHO HAST CREATED MAN FROM EARTH TO REFLECT THINE OWN IMAGE AND LIKENESS, WHO HAS CREATED ME ALSO, UNWORTHY AS I AM, DEIGN, I PRAY THEE, TO BLESS THIS WATER THAT IT MAY BE HEALTHFUL TO MY BODY AND SOUL, THAT ALL DELUSION AND ILL WILL MAY DEPART FROM ME. O LORD GOD, ALMIGHTY AND INEFFABLE , WHO DIDST LEAD THY PEOPLE FORTH FROM THE LAND OF EGYPT, AND DIDST CAUSE THEM TO PASS DRYSHOD OVER THE RED SEA! GRANT THAT I MAY BE CLEANSED BY THIS WATER FROM ALL MY IMPIETIES AND MAY APPEAR BLAMELESS BEFORE THEE. AMEN.

Immerse yourself in the water and imagine all mental and physical impurities washed away.

Approach the altar and invoke Legba/Eshu. Ask for an introduction to the spirits and the ability to speak with them. Use the techniques of self-hypnosis to open yourself to this. Then retire to bed. Keep a dream diary for the night.

This same technique can be performed in the morning, asking for signs of the spirit's presence. This sounds deceptively simple, but if you pursue it for a month or more, you will be startled by the results.

A word of warning: you should be prepared to have experiences that may prove frightening, but if you have the courage to endure these, you will find yourself greatly rewarded and your life changed for the better.

# New Falcon Publications
## Publisher of Controversial Books and CDs
### Invites You to Visit Our Website:
### http://www.newfalcon.com

At the Falcon website you can:

- Browse the online catalog of all our great titles, including books by Robert Anton Wilson, Christopher S. Hyatt, Israel Regardie, Aleister Crowley, Timothy Leary, Osho, Lon Milo DuQuette and many more
- Find out what's available and what's out of stock
- Get special discounts
- Order our titles through our secure online server
- Find products not available anywhere else including:
    - One of a kind and limited availability products
    - Special packages
    - Special pricing
- And much, much more

Get online today at http://www.newfalcon.com